# Using It While Losing It

# Using It While Losing It

*Irving and Suzanne Sarnoff*

iUniverse, Inc.
New York  Lincoln  Shanghai

# Using It While Losing It

iUniverse books may be ordered through booksellers or by contacting:

iUniverse
2021 Pine Lake Road, Suite 100
Lincoln, NE 68512
www.iuniverse.com
1-800-Authors (1-800-288-4677)

Note to Reader: The names of some people in these stories have been changed to protect their identities.

ISBN-13: 978-0-595-34290-7
ISBN-10: 0-595-34290-6

Printed in the United States of America

# *Contents*

# HIGH IN THE SADDLE

Early in the 1980s, while on sabbatical at our house in the Berkshires, we got a call from the producer of the David Letterman Show. We were between books—a trackless terrain where the thrill of soaring inspiration alternates unpredictably with the utter despair of being creatively blocked. On the day we heard from her, we were feeling neither up nor down—just totally blah. That's the way we reacted after picking up our separate phones.

She identified herself as the former producer of the talk show we'd been on in Boston to promote our book about the psychology of masturbation. Perhaps she figured that an aging academic couple, who had been willing to discuss such a subject on TV, would be a perfect pair of freaks to boost Letterman's ratings. We had heard he was being tried out as a possible replacement for Johnny Carson. What could be better than a kinky segment on the carnal mysteries of self-love?

The producer started the conversation by flattering us about how great we had been in Boston and how marvelous we would be in New York. Then she asked what we were "into" now. The expectant catch in her voice suggested she was hoping to find us probing the depths of bestiality or necrophilia.

Hearing we were doing a book on love-centered marriage, she maintained her ingratiating tone and pretended to be fascinated. "Wonderful," she purred. "You can talk about love, marriage… whatever. When would you like to do it?"

Her question stymied us. After suffering brutally from the media tour that brought us to her attention, we were wary about getting on the Tube again. Yet the prospect was very tempting. Unable to make a snap decision, we said we wanted more time to consider her invitation.

When we got off the phone, Irv passed the buck to Sue. "So what do you think?"

"I don't know. It's a lot of stress."

"But Letterman is a rising star."

"What's in it for us? We don't even have a book hot off the press to push."

"Yeah. She sounded desperate to corral any live body she can get. He needs a lot of human props to fill up an hour-and-a-half slot every weekday morning."

"Why torment ourselves just to be seen with him?"

"But it might actually give us a shot in the arm and stimulate our creative juices to flow."

"You could be right." Sue's eyes showed a flicker of enthusiasm. "Maybe going on the show wouldn't be so heavy."

"It's a great opportunity to get across our ideas about deepening love in marriage. After all, we're slaving to package what we have to say in a book."

"So on what logical grounds can we turn down a chance to reach a national audience of a couple of million people?"

Irv smiled. "Obviously, the answer is none."

Having talked ourselves into the gig, we called the producer and set up our appearance for two weeks ahead. She agreed to pay for our travel expenses, including an overnight stay in a hotel in midtown Manhattan.

We began to prepare for a stellar presentation, although feeling ashamed of how much time went into that process. It comforted us, subsequently, to learn that Letterman arrived in his office to psyche himself up five hours before facing the camera.

The hardest part of our preparation was selecting which of our many notions to convey. Not knowing how much time the producer would give us, we came into New York with more material than could be covered if we had the whole program to ourselves. But we wanted to emphasize our basic theme: Mates don't have to lose the romance and pleasure they shared as newlyweds. By giving their relationship proper care, they can strengthen their love and remain passionate companions for a lifetime.

After a tense but not completely sleepless night at the hotel, we walked over to the NBC studios at Rockefeller Center. Arriving long before the scheduled time, we took a detour into the coffee shop on the ground floor. Seating ourselves fitfully, we looked up to see a familiar face in a nearby booth. What a surprise! It was the lawyer we had hired to handle negotiations for the contract on our first book. He was delighted to see us and introduced his wife, who had just finished pitching her latest book on the Today Show.

The coincidence fired us up with tawdry dreams of glory. Wow, we're really in the spotlight of Mediaville!

Seeing and being seen by all the movers and shakers. Hey, a publisher could catch us on Letterman and make us a fabulous offer. Or maybe the executives checking him out will rush down from their lofty observation posts to sign us up for a show of our own.

Already departing from reality and entering the altered state of deluded egoism that television thrives on, we floated into the reception area for Letterman's guests. The producer greeted us with an effusion of lies about how terrific we looked before ushering us to the makeup room. Our hair was styled and cheeks powdered by specialists who worked with jaded finesse. The weariness of their chatter indicated they were beyond being impressed by anyone they had to groom.

Staring at ourselves in a wall of mirrors, we felt like antique mannequins being dusted off for a window display. We were assailed by a gnawing sense of how bizarre it was for us to be here. How low could we sink? Pretty low, we concluded, giving each other faint smiles of commiseration.

We walked into the talent room and sat down before a monitor tuned to the ongoing show. Sprawled in a lounge chair, another guest was watching. Lanky, mustached, and morose, he told us he was a knife thrower. Itching to become a target for instant fame, he muttered solemnly, "This is my big chance."

"Good luck," Irv said, his eyes swimming toward the screen.

Letterman was victimizing a slight and somewhat pedantic man who had developed a technique for using jingles to teach foreign languages. Urged to sing on a stroll around the large set, the unsuspecting sacrifice had his back to the live audience. Meanwhile, Letterman winked into the camera and poured out a poisonous spray of derision at the man's obvious befuddlement. Irv gave Sue a sharp poke. "Do you see that? Letterman is picking him to pieces and the audience is howling!"

"Poor guy."

"It's like Romans feeding Christians to the lions. We'll be out there in ten minutes. We can't let him do that to us."

"But how can we stop him?"

"We can leave now and write the whole thing off as a waking nightmare."

Sue gritted her teeth. "Stop kidding! Let's go think of something."

Staggering into the hallway, we sputtered incoherently for a few minutes. Just as time was running out, we managed to come up with a strategy to save ourselves. We would try to keep him from talking. After he asked his opening question, one of us would answer. The other would pick up the thread before Letterman could resume his interrogation, which we had just seen could be loaded with booby traps and guided missiles.

Although feeling a bit more secure with the invention of our own secret weapon, we were still very jumpy when the producer gave us a last minute briefing. She might keep us on for two segments. It all depended on the reaction of the live audience. If they went dead on our arrival, she would feed Letterman questions to get us through one segment.

Chagrined at having cranked up our stage fright, she earnestly declared, "Not to worry. You'll be O.K." Then, she gently nudged us through the studio door and into Letterman's lair.

Entering to a lively round of applause, whatever sanity we had left was drowned in a swirling bath of adrenaline. We were so pumped up, we couldn't feel our panic.

Letterman loomed before us like a grinning monster, baring his teeth for a tasty kill. But he was surprisingly benign in his introduction. Perhaps he had already gorged himself and needed a rest for digestion. He even seemed content to tolerate our scheme for throwing the conversational ball back and forth between us.

However, he was not entirely disarmed. After a minute of our *shtick*, he decided to stalk us for a vulnerable place to attack. Blandly, he asked about when we got married. As soon as Sue said it was Thanksgiving Day, 1946, he sprang for our juggler veins.

"Thanksgiving?" he sneered, arching his eyebrows to get a rise out of the audience.

Sue responded at once. "Yes, and believe it or not, David, we've been thankful ever since."

The audience exploded with applause—laughing with us not at us—and making Letterman look foolish. Inadvertently, Sue had become the comic, and he had turned into the straight man.

Embarrassed by this reversal, he tried no more offensive forays for the remainder of the segment. Feeling more relaxed, we managed to cover the points we had wanted to make.

At the commercial break, the producer rushed out to say we were going over well and would be kept on for another segment. As we glowed in her praise, Letterman's eyes clouded up with uncertainty. No longer acting larger than life, he put himself in our hands by asking what our focus should be in the next segment. He also exposed his own vulnerability by confessing—without a trace of flippancy—that he knew practically nothing about either love or marriage.

Pulling a small stack of index cards from his jacket, Irv played the part of Letterman's benevolent Dad and said it would be good for us to specify how a couple could develop their loving relationship over all the stages of a lifelong marriage. Nodding his assent, Letterman gave us the green light to proceed.

As we delivered our message, he was on our side all the way. Sympathetically, he even posed a few questions to help us clarify unusual aspects of our perspective. We were only getting started, it seemed, when the second segment ended. Shaking hands with Letterman, who thanked us graciously, we disappeared into the wings.

The producer passed us on her way to prep another guest. From the flatness of her greeting, it was clear she already regarded us as ancient history. Stopping her in mid-stride, we reminded her to send us the check for our expenses.

It took several days to slow down from our speedy state. Appearing before so many viewers had boggled our bodies as well as our minds. What if we had bombed? What if all those people had cast us into oblivion by clicking off their sets?

But weren't we just as worried about filling up the seats in our lecture hall at NYU? Striving to keep our act so lively that students would prefer us to our competitors? Wouldn't the head of our department scuttle the courses we taught together if our enrollments dropped below the profit margin?

Admittedly, universities are more genteel than the television networks. But the bottom-line message to performers is identical. Do whatever it takes to make money or get off the stage.

We could appreciate the plight of David Letterman. The poor bastard puts himself on the block every day. No wonder he has built an arsenal to defend himself against the public guillotine constantly poised above his neck. After putting ourselves at the same risk of execution, we felt lucky to have escaped with only a case of galloping jitters.

Gradually regaining our normal level of nervousness, we let ourselves feel good about coming through for each other and resumed our writing with zest. Maybe the brush with real danger in New York had reduced our tendency to quake from imaginary criticism.

About a month later, there was mail from Letterman's office. Oh, we recalled, on seeing the envelope, this must be the payment for our expenses. We were right. Printed across the top of the check was the name of his company: Space Age Meat.

Irv laughed. "How cynical can a person get?"

"Don't knock him. At least he's honest enough to tell it like it is."

"That's true. Everyone on TV is fair game for the audience to devour. These days, the meat is even being served up on satellite dishes."

"Well, I guess we gave them a couple of pretty good hams to chew on."

# SLINKING INTO SENIORITY

Wobbling under the weight of the briefcases slung over our shoulders, we left the elevator and trudged toward our office. We had just finished a particularly distasteful day of lecturing and were craving to get backstage for some private moaning and groaning

Irv flopped into the creaking swivel chair behind the metal desk. "Perfect planning, right? AIDS before noon and children of divorce after lunch."

Slumping in a plastic arm chair opposite him, Sue smirked. "We sure did get them to think fondly about making love and getting married. If we were really smart, we would have squeezed in a couple of other appetizing topics."

"Yeah, like incest in the sex class and…"

"Domestic violence in the marriage class."

"Right on!" Irv held out his hand for a high-five slap. "That way, we'd have everybody totally wiped out."

"Well, we did a good job on them anyway."

"And on ourselves, too."

Giving way to our fatigue, we stopped talking. Stretching and puffing, we let ourselves feel the pockets of strain in our legs and arms; in the pits of our bellies; in the furrows across our brows. Sue put her glasses on the desk and cupped her hands over her eyes.

Irv let out a jaw-snapping yawn. "Teaching used to be a lot more fun."

"You mean before we had to become the sex police and hand out so many warnings about AIDS and the rest of those charming diseases."

"Yes, but also before teaching anything got to feel like so much work. Haven't you noticed me sitting on the edge of the table while you talk? I can't even stand in one spot for more than ten minutes without getting a cramp in the small of my back."

"What about the pain I still get from the broken metatarsal in my foot?"

"But you've got too much vanity to wear the orthopedic shoes the doctor prescribed."

"Would you like to be up there with those clodhoppers on?"

"I guess not. It would spoil the illusion of us as perennial undergrads."

"Come off it! They may think we're cute...for our age. But we're not fooling them."

"Time sure is a bitch, isn't it, Sue?"

"Let's not get sexist, Irv. Time is a son-of-a-bitch."


Like Carl Sandburg's poetic description of fog, old age creeps up on little cat's feet. Moment by moment, it does its damage within the sound-proofed walls of our bodily cells. Sometimes, the stealthy plundering accumulates enough amplitude to break through the threshold of our hearing. It tolls for us in the rising decibels of the snorts we emit before falling asleep. It calls for attention in the gasping breaths we take as we ascend a flight of stairs. It lets off a mournful wail in the sighs of despair we vent on noticing a cluster of varicose veins sprouting on a flabby stretch of thigh.

Who wants to listen to these dreadful fanfares of advancing deterioration? Surely, not us. We promptly inserted earplugs of denial to shut them out. We also tried to keep those bone-jarring notes from others—the better to mute them from ourselves.

But these defenses failed to spare us the agonies of our aging. Irv was troubled by hemorrhoids and got indigestion from spicy foods. Tiring more quickly than he did a few years ago, he began to regard lecturing as a form of menial labor. How could he continue to pull his weight in carrying our heavy load of teaching and writing?

Sue voiced shrill alarms at the painful arthritic lumps expanding on her knuckles. She was equally upset by the numbness invading her fingers from the traffic jam in the carpal tunnels in her wrists. These ailments seriously threatened her ability to type. And while Irv was disturbed by his constipation, she worried about the frequency of her nocturnal trips to the toilet.

For a while, we thought we could deal with our concerns by following the precepts of Eastern philosophy. If we could fully accept the inexorable process of aging, we might attain a transcendent feeling of oneness with our changes. Then we could fasten our mental seat belts and ride joyfully with the wintry winds blowing through us. By embracing this attitude, we would reach the end of our lifetime—aches, infirmities, and all—optimally fulfilled and ready to make room for someone else to embark on the same fantastic journey. In other words, be here now and go with the flow.

Fine. We made fairly good use of this wisdom when Irv was only 60 and Sue was 54. Although prey to flashes of anxiety about growing old, we could easily immerse ourselves in the hereness and nowness of whatever was transpiring inside or outside of us. Heeding the testimonies of Baba Ram Dass, Irv cultivated the art of melting into his increasingly bony butt for the better part of a day. Sue learned to sit just as serenely on her billowing buttocks. Side by side, we merged with the changing nuances of color and texture as the sun set on the patch of the Hudson River we could see from our apartment.

But now, with Irv 65 and Sue 59, we encountered a steely inner resistance whenever we tried to emulate the equanimity of the Buddha. How could we feel great about going with the flow when it was getting closer to stopping? How could we cheerfully blend with our bliss when it was rapidly flushing us down the same hole where we piss?

As psychologists, we were acquainted with the geriatric literature describing how elderly people complain about their plight. Previously, these accounts seemed irrelevant to us. Today, we were Exhibit A ourselves.

"Whatever we call it, Sue, the passage of time is something we'll have to accept."

Getting up, she began to sort the papers scattered on the desk. "But that's not enough. We have to lighten our load. Knocking ourselves out pretending we're younger has only been making us feel older."

"But there's no way we can stop what's happening to us."

Moving around the desk, she tweaked Irv under the chin. "If we can't stop it, we don't want to do anything. Do we?"

"O.K., O.K., easing up isn't the same as giving up." He gently stroked her thigh. "We'll never stop making love…even when we become too wasted for anything else."

She nestled into his lap. "Isn't that the whole point? If we wear ourselves out too much, the only thing we'll be able to do in bed is sleep."

"God forbid!"

"We can't stop time…but we can decide how to use what's left to us."

"You're right. We have to let go while still holding on. But that's a hard stunt to pull off."

The ringing telephone startled us. Sue jumped up and lunged for the receiver. "Oh, yes? We've been waiting to hear from you. Oh? That's too bad." Waving frantically at Irv, who was squirming in his seat, she pointed to the copy of our manuscript sitting on the top of the file cabinet. "I hope you're feeling better now."

Unable to contain himself, Irv whispered hoarsely, "What's up?"

Ignoring him, Sue smiled into space. "That's very nice news. When do you think you'll come to a final decision?"

"What?" he demanded again.

She glared at him but kept talking. "In a week? You can reach us here in the office…the answering machine is on when nobody's around. Or should we phone you?"

While Irv went ape with impatience, Sue remained calm and cordial. "Thanks so much. We'll be looking forward to your call. And…and stay well."

Hanging up, she let out a whoop. "Wow! It was the editor from the publishing house. They're really interested in our book. I mean really!"

"What did she say?"

"First of all, she didn't get back to us sooner because she had a relapse of pneumonia and was in the hospital for the last two weeks. But her outside reader recommended that they publish it. He liked our approach to marriage. All she needs now is approval from the editorial board. But she said it looks good." Sue took a deep breath. "She's very enthusiastic about working with us. When it's definite, she'll be in touch. She didn't want us to call her."

"Of course not! That was a stupid thing for you to ask. You made us look too anxious."

"Oh, stop it! I was freaking out of my mind after all this suspense. And the way you were bugging me in the background. You wouldn't have handled it any better."

Jumping up, Irv kissed her impulsively and twirled her around the room. "What the hell are we fighting about? This is what we've been waiting to hear!"

For almost a year, we had been sending our manuscript to publishers. Several senior editors liked it a lot.

But they couldn't generate enough support among their colleagues. One editor-in-chief said he would accept it if we took out our social and political critique.

Our bitterest disappointment came in the aftermath of a call from the executive editor of a large trade house. On the telephone, he showered us with superlatives. Our book was exactly what he had been looking for—a refreshing contrast to all the "popcorn" on this important topic. He was definitely going to publish it and we would soon be getting a letter with a formal offer.

A month passed before we heard from him. His letter was a voluminous apology. He had changed his mind since speaking to us. Although he had the greatest respect for the quality of our work, in the last analysis "it wasn't quite right for his list."

Sue put an abrupt end to our dancing. "Let's hope this isn't just a big tease, like the others we've had."

"Don't be such a worry wart! It's nice to have something positive to look forward to."

"Look who's cheering us on now."

"I'm finally letting myself be optimistic for a change. Why don't we get out of here and do something to celebrate."

"Well, the movie we've been wanting to see goes on in twenty minutes. We can still make it. But let's not slip on any banana peels getting there."

Levitating through Washington Square Park, we turned down West Third Street and headed toward Sixth Avenue. Nearing the Waverly, Sue brought us down to earth. "You know, it's not five o'clock yet. You could get a ticket at the rate for seniors."

"What?"

"You know what. You've got your Medicare Card. Why not use it for the discount you're entitled to?"

"Haven't I had enough excitement for one day? What are you trying to do...give me a heart attack?"

"I thought you were ready to stop playing games with yourself. It's crazy to spend more money than we have to."

"O.K., so I'm a Senior Citizen. But I don't have to make a public announcement about it. I doubt that you would."

"I thought we just agreed to take a more realistic approach to our age. Don't forget..."

Suddenly, Sue went speechless. What's going on with me? Why am I needling him? He's right. I'd be just as reluctant to admit I was 65. The six years between us gives me a temporary reprieve. But the social security system will be administering the same jolt of shock therapy to me. Will I react any better? Maybe getting on Irv's back is a sneaky way of stroking my own ego...making me seem so young. Or maybe I'm trying to force *myself* to do a little more reality-testing.

Sue softened. "Honey, I can understand..."

Irv bolted away from her. He came to a halt at the box office and glowered at the sign listing the prices of admission. Adults: $7.00; Children and Seniors: $4.00. Pale and twitching, he blurted out, "One adult and one senior."

The cashier hit the buttons for the two tickets and put them on the counter. She didn't say, "Oh, no, you must be kidding. You, a senior? Don't make me laugh!" She didn't even ask to see his Medicare Card or any other ID.

Holding the money in his hand, Irv kept waiting for the cashier to challenge him. But she didn't.

Meekly, he handed over a twenty dollar bill, pocketed the change, and picked up the tickets. Entering the theater, he shuffled along the aisle behind Sue and sat down in the seat she chose for him.

"You were great! I hope I can do as well when my turn comes around."

"No problem," he sighed. "You know us seniors. We'd admit to anything to get a bargain."

# CAGED BY THE RAGE AGAINST AGE

From down the hall, the rising euphoria of the party seeped under the door of our apartment. We could hear Nina's gleeful shrieks as she welcomed guests to her annual spring bash. The bartender had already come to get more of the champagne we had been keeping on ice for her.

Delaying our own appearance at the affair, Irv knotted his tie for the third time and frowned at the mirror. Sue pulled off the sweater she had decided to change in favor of a silk blouse. Both of us were upset because we liked to be on time. We had been looking forward to goofing with Nina as we always did in random encounters in the elevator or on the street. So why were we dawdling in dread of a situation made-to-order for being zany?

True, these cocktail parties are laced with tension, as people compare their projects and prospects. Since Nina is in a different department, we wouldn't know most of the hotshots there. But we had never been shy of strangers—when we had something to crow about.

However, we were sitting on news that couldn't possibly impress anyone she would have on hand. In another month, we would no longer be employed at NYU or anywhere else. Struggling to digest this fact for almost a year, we hadn't announced it to anyone.

Irv stopped fidgeting and ventilated our nagging distress. "Typical cases, right? Rusty nails from Freud's iron law of ambivalence. First, we push for early retirement. Then we reject the University's severance deal as too miserly."

"Luckily they refused to give us the health benefits we asked for. That gave us a good excuse to cop out. We really wanted to stay on until you turn seventy next month."

"What a paradox. I'm a full professor and the law forces me to retire at seventy. You're just an adjunct lecturer but they would have let you teach our courses on your own. Of course, you're only sixty-four."

"Well, it was nice of them to make me the offer."

"Why shouldn't they? You and I created those courses. The first ones the psychology department ever offered on sex and marriage."

"Even though I could have continued on my own, you know damn well we wouldn't split up after teaching as a team for twelve years."

"Maybe, it's just as well. We can't deny how much we've hated to repeat the same material over and over again. I know we tried to keep ourselves interested by relating the topics to whatever was going on culturally and politically. But it didn't dispel our escalating boredom."

"The thing I hated most was having to give exams. Who could stand all that vicious competition for grades? Every time we handed back a test, we were bombarded by flak from a bunch of kids who were ready to kill to get a B+ changed to an A-."

"Still, if I didn't have to retire, we'd probably stick to the same old routine, like toddlers clinging to a security blanket."

Bracing ourselves, we left our apartment and walked the few steps over to Nina's place. Entering hesitantly, we pushed through the tightly packed crowd. Our nervousness clearly clashed with the self-congratulatory aura surrounding us.

Noticing us from afar, Nina waved and wove her way toward us. A prominent figure in the Tisch School of the Arts, she was arrestingly costumed in a Chinese satin tunic and flowing trousers. Her ebony hair was dyed to a glistening sheen and perfectly cropped in a fashionable wedge. After a welcoming hug, she took us to the bar and left us there alone. Tonight, she was strictly business.

While sipping our drinks, we checked out the scene. Most of the men and women were senior members of the faculty. Nina's friends from the "outside world" of film, TV, and the theater contributed panache to the scintillating ambiance she had staged. And several gung-ho graduate students gave the proceedings a charge of youthful promise.

Milling about, we searched in vain for a familiar face. Jostled from one clump of luminaries to another, we felt increasingly intimidated by the tidbits we overheard.

"How was your book tour?"

"Terrific! It couldn't have gone better."

"I happened to tune into NPR on my way home from work. And there you were! You really came across very well."

Moving to the margin of another group, we picked up similar smatterings of success.

"The play is moving to Broadway."

"A producer just bought an option on my film script."

For almost thirty years, we had lived and worked in this creative core of The Big Apple. Our building is a faculty residence designed by I.M. Pei, the architect who later did an addition to the Louvre. A gigantic replica of a statue by Picasso watches over the entrance to our vaulting beehive, which straddles the boundary of Soho and Greenwich Village.

The neighborhood is filled with writers, artists, actors, and scholars. Every year, a fresh crop of bright wannabes appears, driven by the dream of "making it." With such a concentration of talent and ambition, the area generates a torrent of new trends, most of which eventually trickle into the mindset of the rest of the country. It was easy for us to see ourselves as busy contributors to this vital nexus of invention.

Our contributions were quite respectable. The book we wrote on marriage came out a few years ago to good reviews. We also did an article based on it for Psychology Today.

But for months, we'd been harassing each other with different ideas about what we would write next. With nothing new in the works, we felt ashamedly out of it in this milieu, where the only thing that matters is what you're accomplishing at the moment.

Privately, we had been telling each other we wished for nothing more than a simple life in the woods of our beloved Berkshires. Settling down in the country had always been a basic element of our retirement plans.

Kicking the urban rat race, we would mellow out in our cozy house. There, surrounded by peace and quiet, we would have the serenity to plumb our creative depths. But now that this possibility was within our grasp, we were shrinking away from it.

Retreating to an unoccupied niche near the huge windows, Sue scanned the panoramic view of lower Manhattan. "The picture we see looking uptown from our own living room is just as gorgeous. We'll miss it."

"But you've been complaining about the work it takes to keep up our large apartment."

"I know. We don't need all that space anymore…just for the two of us. But it doesn't feel good to be forced to vacate a place where we've spent some of our best years."

Sue's comment cast us into a wistful reverie. The Village! The very thought of being here had always sent shivers up and down our spines. It was our Promised Land from the time we started going together in Flatbush at the end of World War II. How eagerly we anticipated our heavy dates on Saturdays, when we had the leisure to spend all day—and most of the night— soaking up the bohemian atmosphere of the area, which epitomized daring and originality for us.

We entered marriage with Greenwich Village branded in our brains as *the* place to be. But we didn't get to live here for another twenty-two years. In the interim, we went on an academic circuit from Brooklyn to Ann Arbor, London, New Haven, and Cleveland. In 1962, when Irv got a job at NYU, we returned to Brooklyn, where we took shelter for several years until our son and daughter were old enough for us to feel secure about moving into Manhattan. After taking root on Bleecker Street, we felt we had made the romantic dream of our youth come true.

Irv looked into Sue's eyes. "Maybe we had an overre-action, thinking we could let go of the city entirely and spend all of our time in the country."

"You're not the first one to say that. Whenever we've glorified our sabbaticals in the Berkshires, our friends there said we felt that way because we knew we'd be going back to New York."

"I've given thirty years to this university," Irv grum-bled, "and they haven't even given me a gold watch. But now, they're offering us a studio in Washington Square Village. I know it's only a booby prize for giving up our big apartment. Why not take advantage of it? If it was good enough for Anais Nin in her old age, it should be good enough for us."

"I guess you're right. And we'll never have another chance to get one at such a reasonable rent."

A commanding voice snapped our attention away from the twin towers of the World Trade Center. It was Bob Thompson, a sociologist we knew. A solid citizen who had gotten lucrative grants, he had written a stan-dard text and his research papers were published in the most prestigious journals.

"Nice to see you!" he bellowed, approaching us. The icy glint in his blue eyes was somewhat softened by the smile that ruffled the well-trimmed lines of his gray goatee. "How are you folks these days?"

"Fine...fine," we said in unison.

"You must be feeling good about yourselves. Everyone in my department is amazed by the enrollment you've gotten in your marriage class. We knew your sex course was popular. Sex always sells. But you're getting them to buy monogamy, too!"

"Yeah, we've done a take off on McLuhan," Irv snickered. "Our medium is our message."

"I'm fascinated by your duet. My wife and I would get divorced if we tried it. How do you manage?"

"With difficulty...when we started. We often competed for the limelight and fought about what should be covered. Now," Irv quickly added, "we can laugh at ourselves."

"Do you take turns lecturing on different topics?"

"Oh, no," Sue said. "Both of us are always up there yakking."

"Of course, we come in with notes," Irv explained. "But we add or subtract things on the spot. What we enjoy most is the spontaneity of fielding questions from the floor."

"I'll give an answer and Irv will chime in with more information...or vice versa. Sometimes, we even disagree. But the students like to see us argue. It reminds them of their parents...or a soap opera."

Thompson laughed. "Sounds like a TV talk show. Are you offering both courses next semester?"

This was it! The direct question we had been hoping to avoid. "Well..." Irv stuttered, "we've been doing them every term...but...we're... we're retiring at the end of this academic year."

"Oh? Really?" Thompson squinted in troubled surprise. "What are you going to do?"

"We want to focus our energies on writing," Sue chirped, failing at an attempt to smile.

"Excellent!" His feigned enthusiasm reflected an underlying attitude of pity and condescension.

We were stunned by the put-down. Thompson stared intently beyond us for an opportunity to escape. Only a few years younger than Irv, his abrupt emotional withdrawal seemed to be saying: "There but for the grace of God go I."

Seeing we were already dead in his eyes, we backed off and pretended to want another drink. Trembling, we walked toward the bar. Incredibly, we had underestimated the horrendous effect of the "R" word. Like a satanic curse, it transformed us from a highly admired campus couple to a pair of pathetic has-beens strewn on a slag heap.

Thompson's reaction exceeded our worst fears. For us, the party was definitely over. Mumbling our goodbyes to Nina, we fled to the sanctuary of our own apartment.

Collapsing on the sofa, we gawked at the vastness of the city. At the thrusting spires and masses of stone. At the Empire State Building, its phallic shaft piercing the sky like a mythical totem erected to the spirit of limitless aspiration.

"How did you like the way Thompson blanched when we told him we were leaving?"

"The hell with him!" Irv fumed. "We may be retiring but we're not expiring."

Yet we had to admit that our days were numbered. With graying hair, sagging jowls, and wrinkles that could not be washed away, we had traveled far down the one-way street of No Return.

This awareness haunted and taunted us. It had become a pervasive and maddening presence—constantly poised to leap into the forefront of our consciousness with a ghastly cackle at any creative project we might envision. Did we still have the marbles to do it? Even if we did, would we stay alive long enough to complete it?

Enraged, we felt trapped in a prison where all we could do was beat our seething skulls against invisible bars. We knew everyone faced the same fate. But why *us*? Why couldn't we be granted some special dispensation for good behavior—a providential pardon that would release us with a guarantee of no more damage than we had already endured?

In this agitated state, we fully empathized with the anguished protest of Dylan Thomas:

> *Do not go gentle into that good night,*
> *Old age should burn and rage at the close of day;*
> *Rage, rage against the dying of the light.*

But raging can go too far, turning back and assaulting the enraged rather than the object of their anger. Excessively offended by the limits of mortality, Dylan Thomas wound up a victim of his own indignation. Cutting off his life to spite his death, he drank himself into a very early grave. Surely, we didn't have to act out the idiotic irony of defying the Grim Reaper by doing ourselves in long before he was ready to mow us down.

"There's no doubt," Sue moaned, "that getting old is a double whammy for us. It's reminding us that our whole life trip is winding down and it's pushing us out of our academic trip."

"Yeah, our hit show is ending its long run."

"It was a lovely romance while it lasted." She sank into the pillows. "Look, the stage of life we're going through now throws everyone into a tizzy. Remember the mid-life crisis?"

"No, I don't. It happened too long ago."

"Poor old man. I feel so sorry for you. But I won't let you off the hook. You'll have to cope with this one, too."

"It's going to be a lot tougher. You're not exactly Ms. High Voltage anymore, either."

"Cut the whining. Nobody's going to do it for us."

"Right. From now on, when we go to a party, let's just tell people we're making a career change."

# SURVEYED INTO SATORI

Squeezed into a narrow corridor of the Town Hall, a large crowd grumbled about the heat of the August afternoon. Overcome, some people had to step outside for a breath of air, losing their precious places on line. But nobody went home. The occasion was too important. We had been invited to see how the newly completed land map of the town matched our own records of the size and borders of our property. From now on, this map was going to be the official basis for levying real estate taxes.

Moving close to the anteroom where the assessor held court, we could see and hear James Cahill, an investment banker with a major firm in New York, who owned an eyebrow colonial set high on a sprawling hill. While trying to maintain a dignified facade, he couldn't suppress his agitation on learning that his holdings had shrunk drastically.

"But that parcel I bought across the road for protection from developers was supposed to be 125 acres—not 67!" His intense blue eyes flashed with hysteria and the translucent skin on his hawkish nose tightened around his dilating nostrils. "I paid the price for 125. Do you mean to tell me I was taken?"

John Martin, the assessor, ran his stubby fingers through the damp mat of gray hair above his weather-beaten brow. "Don't know, Mr. Cahill. We just go by what they show us."

"Well, they're not going to get away with it," Cahill hissed, glowering at everyone as he whirled around and left the room.

Mary Lee Quinn sprang forward to take his place. Bedecked in a grimy pink sweat suit, she pressed all of her 200 pounds against the desk. "My lot was exactly one acre. That's what I've been paying taxes on for thirty years." A bolt of rage pierced her booming voice. "Are you saying I own two acres?"

Martin kept his head lowered, scanning the drawing of her land. "Well, it says right here…"

"I know you guys don't give anything away!"

"It's not us, Mary. We…"

"Goddamn it, I still have the same piece of dirt! Why the hell should I pay twice as much taxes for it?"

Letting her question vibrate in the stifling atmosphere, Mary waited for an answer. When Martin sighed and glanced at the restless throng, she snorted loudly and stomped off.

Thoroughly shaken, we cringed as he waved us forward. With a resentful look at the diagram we were shown, Irv whined, "This isn't the right parcel. Our place is 23 acres. The number here is only 14.3."

Sue grabbed his shoulder. "Of course it's ours, honey. Don't you see the diamond shape of the land and the Clam River along its southwest boundary? The picture is right…but there must be some mistake about the acreage."

Since Martin was a neighbor of ours, Sue smiled, trying hard to be cordial. But her tone was spiked with distrust. "Are these drawings based on actual surveys?"

Martin squirmed. "No…but the consultants used very accurate aerial photos. I'm pretty sure these guys know what they're doing."

"Well, I'm not! They definitely got the numbers wrong about our place."

"Is this information legal?" Irv demanded.

"Not really," Martin admitted, "only a surveyor's findings would hold up in court."

Stumbling out of the door, we shielded our eyes against the fiery sun. But we couldn't dampen the blaze of our self-recrimination. "Some hip city slickers," Irv fumed. "We didn't even have the sense to get our land surveyed. Just accepted the deed as if it had been handed down to us by Moses."

"We should have known better when we saw that slimy phrase 'more or less' written after the 23 acres."

"And we sure were shrewd to have the same lawyer as the sellers. Another attorney might have advised us to find out exactly how much land we were buying."

Sue nodded her head sadly. "We probably could have gotten fourteen acres for thousands less than we paid. Especially since the Simons did nothing to conceal how eager they were to make a sale."

As we crossed the bridge over the river between our house and the main road, both of us stopped at the same instant, captivated by the golden light shimmering on the swiftly flowing water. This gorgeous view was our constant delight. Yet we had the gall to complain about being ripped off by the cartographers. What was happening to us? Had we become as rapacious as the colonists who founded our township?

According to local legend, our town was bought from the Indians in the middle of the 1700s for three barrels of rum and thirty quarts of cider. Undoubtedly, with their guns at the ready, the colonists would have taken the land for free if the Indians had turned down their offer. But the barter was still a steal for the settlers, given what they got for their firewater: 52 square miles of the beautiful Berkshires. All the Indians could possibly have gotten was a giant hangover.

This history exemplifies the methods used to rob the entire country from the Native Americans. Eventually, the European conquerors devised a complicated legal system to obscure the criminal origins of their acquisitions. Ever since, the transfer of land from one owner to another has become a more genteel process of expropriation. Now, money—not a musket—is the socially approved weapon for everyone in the market for real estate.

Still, the ownership of private property is protected by the armed power of the State. We have the right to call on the police to drive away anyone who sets foot on our land without explicit permission. It wouldn't matter to the constables whether the trespassers were tipsy deer hunters or a famished family scrounging for rotten apples under the gnarled trees of our abandoned orchard.

Of course, we would never refuse to feed anyone we found starving on our land. But what if a band of marauders were prepared to kill us and seize our property?

Unlike our neighbors, who are well equipped to serve as their own security force, we have no guns to fend off intruders. Would we attack them with our bare hands and fight to the death? No way! We'd let them have the place to save our skins. Yet we had become as attached to our land as barnacles to a jetty. So when the new map showed we had nine acres less to cling to, we felt mortally threatened.

Storming into our kitchen, Sue screamed, "We're living in capitalist America—not a utopian commune! Why should we let ourselves be fleeced?"

"That's the agonizing question." Irv plopped onto a stool at the counter and gazed through the bay window above the sink. Admiring the stately blue spruce at the entrance to our driveway, he mused, "We've always agreed with Proudhon that property is theft."

"So we tried to avoid becoming thieves by renting instead of owning. But where did that get us?"

"Not into heaven, that's for sure. It took us twenty years to stop denying ourselves the pleasure of our own home."

"It's not as if we wanted to become landlords and get rich by soaking people with high rents. We just got tired of being exploited ourselves."

Irv stood up and shrugged. "So we broke our ideological taboo."

"You make it sound like losing our virginity."

"Well, weren't we acting like innocents? Maybe we were right from a spiritual perspective. But, like you said, we're living in a material world."

"Yeah, but gloating over the size of our spread makes us feel guilty," Sue conceded. "It feels downright decadent to keep it as our private playpen...especially since we don't do anything with our acreage that people consider useful. We don't even log it or put in a vegetable garden."

"Wait a minute!" Irv yelled. "Look at the books we've written up here. It's our Word Farm."

"You're right. It's the wild beauty that helps to inspire us."

We had always lived in close proximity to other people. The one house we briefly owned in Brooklyn was hemmed in by others of the same design. And our Manhattan apartment was in a tower building that contained over a hundred families.

Country life exposed us to a novel experience. Nestled in the corner of a broad clearing, our house is bounded by the river on one side and, on the other, faces a few small houses set at some distance across a narrow road. But in the back, where the field meanders into the woods, we're surrounded by pristine seclusion. Acre after acre of trees blanket most of our land and that of our abutter.

Fascinated by this isolated setting, we were also intimidated by it. Hesitant to venture into the forest alone, Sue became the "inside" partner, taking on the formidable challenge of making our funky little farm-house more comfortable and appealing. Slipping into the role of "outside man," Irv was secretly overwhelmed by the enormous task of managing the land. He didn't do much but hire someone to mow the grass in summer and plow the snow in winter. It was hiking in the woods and losing himself in its natural glory that gave him the greatest emotional charge.

Over the years, we developed a common ritual for sharing the splendor of our place. Every time we came up from the city, we rushed out to walk over the land. Pacing the perimeter up the steeply rising road, we headed into the woods at the stone wall that bordered the northern boundary of our acreage.

Following the wall as it tumbled precipitously down toward the river, we had to climb over dead logs, circle huge boulders, and push through dense growth of mountain laurel and white pine. At the water's edge, we took a break, marveling at the sights and sounds. Usually, we sat where a teetering wooden post had been planted, we believed, to mark our western border.

Sometimes, we went beyond the post and furtively invaded a spectacular stretch of land along the river, which we assumed was owned by our neighbors. Feeling daring and adventurous, we pushed further up a rocky path that rose sharply above the river bank. Climbing cautiously over rugged slabs of moss-covered ledge, we reached a high bower surrounded by four huge hemlocks that soared upward like columns meant to support the sky itself. At their lofty crowns, they fused together in a mighty canopy of green lace.

Leaning back on the soft bed of pine needles, we looked up from below. Beams of sunlight filtered through the foliage in a pattern of radiance that lit up the darkest recesses of our beings. We seemed to transcend the limits of our everyday selves, experiencing a sense of oneness with all living things. Naming this enthralling refuge, The Dream Place, we returned to it often.

Everyone we've ever brought to that place has been awestruck. Even our grandchildren, who were brave enough as youngsters to make the scary journey with us, had the same reaction. And they still love to go there.


"Whenever we crow about our property," Sue said, "I think we're a couple of sophisticated savages. Look how we reacted today at the Town Hall. Maybe people are driven by an inborn territorial instinct."

"Who knows? But it would be good to find out how much land we actually have in case we're ever forced to sell the place after we retire up here,"

"A real survey will certainly prove those goddamn cartographers are wrong. It could easily turn out that we own *more* than 23 acres—not less!"

We decided to use Tom Reese. Several years ago, he had given us an unexpected windfall from a job he did for Mr. Porter, who lives across the road. From his research, Tom had learned that a narrow, half-acre strip of Mr. Porter's land had originally been part of our parcel.

That piece was included in the acreage Mr. Porter was planning to sell. He was counting on its 200 feet of road frontage to meet the legal requirement for anyone to put a house on it. When he offered to purchase the land from us, we were amazed to learn it was ours.

At first, we were reluctant to part with it. Who knows, we wondered, wouldn't any kind of house destroy the woods facing our property and lower its value? On the other hand, what would be the point of holding on to it? Short of a full acre, it couldn't qualify as a building lot. Besides, we feared Mr. Porter would harbor a lifelong grudge against us if we prevented him from making his deal. So we sold him the piece, hoping whoever bought it from him wouldn't disturb our tranquility.

Ironically, Tom's estimate for doing our survey almost equaled the amount we made from our sale to Mr. Porter. Essentially, we'd be getting a free ride. We took this as a magical sign that it was wise to hire Tom. Perhaps, he would do us another good turn and find that we owned much more than the tax map indicated.

In our first meeting with him, we made it perfectly clear that we felt the cartographers had grossly underestimated our acreage. Listening respectfully, Tom assured us he would do everything necessary to conduct an accurate survey.

About a week later, he appeared for a preliminary inspection. Inviting himself to go along, Irv scurried after him up the road. On the way, Tom said the stone wall cutting into our place was, indeed, the boundary with our abutter to the north. He established this fact on the basis of records he had already examined at the Registry of Deeds. However, as he and Irv followed the wall down through the woods, Tom halted at the point where it abruptly collapsed into a haphazard mound of stones.

Blinking his dark brown eyes, Tom seemed at a loss to know where to proceed. For a while, he just stared at the rotting stump of a maple tree. "The stone wall was the kind of permanent marker people always used around here," he said. "This one points downward in a very straight line…as far as it goes." Then, almost under his breath, he mumbled softly, "I guess the safest bet is to mentally extend the wall as if it descended to the river in the same straight line."

Irv immediately saw that this extension of the wall would put The Dream Place within the borders of our property. Aha, he thought, his brain aflame with land fever, here's a stroke of luck we never even hoped for! If that mystical grove turns out to be a legitimate part of our family holdings, we'll all be able to enjoy dreaming there without feeling like trespassers. Trying to avoid exposing his greed, he asked humbly, "But are you sure, Tom?"

"Well, surveying is based on a lot of precedent and experience," Tom said calmly. "We just do the best we know how."

As Irv scrambled to keep up with Tom's descent through the thickets, he realized how much power is vested in surveyors. These guys aren't mere technicians in regard to property ownership. They're THE LAST JUDGMENT. Reaching the bank, he was thrilled to see the long stretch of river Tom was going to hand over to us. Surely, the final survey was bound to give us more than 23 acres.

During the next few weeks, Tom's assistants repeatedly tramped over our land, setting up their tripods and telescopic instruments, doing their sightings, and getting finely tuned readings. Occasionally, we sneaked into the woods behind them, spying on the trail of red ribbons they had tied to some of the trees. And we exulted silently when we saw them drive a cast iron stake—far beyond the old wooden one—into the spot they calculated was our true western boundary.

Eager as we were to get the official blueprint, we knew it would take a few weeks to prepare. After waiting a month without any word, we became antsy and contacted Tom on the telephone.

"It takes time to nail down all the details. We want to be careful not to make any mistakes."

Given this explanation, we tolerated another month of suspense before stinging bites of paranoia began to itch us. Egging each other on, we thought and talked of nothing else but what the survey would reveal. It was scarcely reassuring to call Tom again, only to be informed he was swamped with work. His evasive attitude incited us to badger each other with more poisonous questions. Why is he putting us off? Could he be setting us up to ask for more money?

Getting in touch with us, at last, Tom made an appointment to deliver the survey.

"Look, he's here!" Sue shouted, spotting him from the kitchen window, a large roll of cardboard tucked under his arm.

Needing no explanation of who "he" was, Irv shot up from his recliner and ran to open the door. "Glad to see you, Tom. It's been a long time."

We shook with impatience as he pulled the blueprint from its sheath and spread it out on the dining room table. Tom quickly drew our attention to the extra triangle of land he had included in our parcel. He emphasized the additional footage we now owned along the southwestern boundary, giving us a quarter of a mile of river front. And he positively glowed as he informed us we also owned the bed *under* the water—all the way to the opposite strand.

Pleasantly surprised, we beamed at each other. But when he moved his hand away from the diagram, we saw the amount—14.3—inscribed in large blue numbers right in the center of the page.

We flipped. This was exactly the same amount the cartographers had listed on the tax map. Could there be some collusion between them and Tom?

"How can this be? How could 23 acres turn into 14.3, just like that?" Sue snapped her fingers accusingly.

Irv vehemently joined her protest. "Yeah, especially with that extra piece that wasn't even on the tax map!"

Trying to appease us, Tom launched into a detailed account. First of all, in researching the line of title during the late 1800s, he found a discrepancy in the number of acres transferred from one deed to another. Whether due to human error or sheer malice, our parcel, which had been 18 acres from the beginning of the century, was described as 23 acres on the next deed. From that time onward, all the subsequent deeds perpetuated the mistake.

"But that's only a difference of five acres," Sue groaned. "What happened to the other four?"

Continuing his discourse, Tom described the primitive procedure once used by surveyors. Working only with a length of iron chain, they repeatedly laid it along the borders to get their measurements. If the land was very hilly, the total figure included all the ups and downs of each slope. Now, however, they base their computations on the flat plane that goes from point to point over the property lines—regardless of the terrain in between. So, it's not unusual to find a steep parcel like ours turn out to be several acres smaller than originally calculated.

His impeccable logic did nothing for our sunken morale. As soon as he was gone, Sue moaned, "We needed it badly. After all the torture and expense, we're right back where we started."

"I guess you could say it was an exercise in complete futility. Of course, we could look at it this way…we still own what we thought we bought in the first place."

"That's true. But who could have imagined it would measure so much less? We were living in fantasy land...thinking Tom would hand us another bonanza."

Suddenly, Irv let out an inane giggle, as if catching on to a strange joke. "Sure, the number of acres *is* smaller. But in terms of the *real land*...the ground we can see and touch and hike through...the place is bigger than it ever was."

Sue smiled weakly. "You mean it's like a Zen koan? More turned out to be less...but less is also more."

"Bingo baby! For the same money, we got enlightenment, too!"

# REARRANGING
# REALITY

We hated those asbestos shingles from the moment we saw our place. Bilious green and creased to simulate cedar shakes, they could set loose toxic fibers if broken or crushed. What damage and decay lay beneath the brittle stiffness of their surface? Surely, as our insurance agent candidly told us, the ersatz facade automatically undermined the charm and value of our eighteenth century farmhouse.

When we bought it, we had vowed to replace the siding with genuine clapboards. But finding some of the rooms in need of repair, we decided to renovate them first. Meanwhile, we pretended the shingles had disappeared from our field of vision. Now, as we sat on the front porch absorbing the aftershocks of recent retirement, all our chickens of neglect came home to roost.

Squirming in our chairs, we also got worked up by the ugliness of the porch. How could we have endured this for twenty years? On all sides, our view was marred by rusty screens crowned by the pitted glass panels of corroded storm windows. Peeling paint left the ceiling blotched with raw scars. The battered door looked as if it had been retrieved from the town dump. Pitched forward in a precarious slant, the floor was indelibly spattered with stains of bat caca in a pattern Jackson Pollack would have admired.

"I'm sick of this!" Sue screeched. "We've got to do whatever it takes to wipe out this blight."

"It's going to take big bucks. But that's nothing new. Remember what the agent in Brooklyn said when we bought our first house?"

That lady was not only an exceptional comedienne but also a world-class oracle. At a crucial juncture in our negotiations, we aired our dismay at what it would cost to repair the damaged stucco on the outside walls. For a quiet moment, she enfolded us in a compassionate gaze worthy of Mother Teresa. Then, switching roles with awesome skill, she gave us Mona Lisa's enigmatic smile and disclosed the secret of home ownership. "What can I tell you? A house is a well."

Despite her warning, we bought the "well." Soon, just as she predicted, we were pumping money into it. By some mysterious Law of Nature, it got a bit deeper. But that fake Dutch Colonial, circa 1930, turned out to be an ordinary well of limited depth. In fact, we made a small profit when we sold it a few years later to move into Manhattan.

However our authentic Colonial in the Berkshires, dating back to the late 1700s, had the word ARTESIAN written in capital letters all over it. We knew it would have to be expanded and redecorated inside and out. Obviously, its capacity to drill for money was going to drain the deepest recesses of our pocketbook.

We could have continued to look for something more sensible. But as soon as we walked behind the house, we lost our senses to a profusion of beauty. On that gleaming day in May, the flowering apple trees on the lush lawn seemed like the portals of Eden. The sky was a silken canopy of azure, the air heady with the scent of blossoms rejoicing at the arrival of spring.

Enchanted by the setting, we were prepared to accept whatever imperfections the house contained. But upon entering, we were pleasantly surprised. The original builders had angled the structure in just the right direction to pick up the best light throughout the day. The sunshine pouring through the windows of the living room made it sparkle like a jewel box. Although the kitchen and bathroom were antiquated, everything was clean and in working order. We could move in at once. It wasn't exactly our "dream house," but compared favorably with some of the run-down shacks we had seen.

Observing our reaction, the real estate agent quickly followed up for the kill. "Would you like to walk the property lines?"

Letting him take the lead, we tramped through the woods, staying close to the Clam River, which marked off the southwestern boundary of the land. The crystalline water seemed to gurgle and coo with contentment. And brook trout swam in pools dammed by clusters of rocks.

Further along the bank, we reached a dramatic fork where the Buck River bubbled and foamed as it rushed rapidly downward to join the Clam. The Silverbrook also flowed into the Clam across the road from the front of the house. Apparently, the land was graced by the confluence of three rivers! How lucky could we get?

From the banks of the Clam a thick forest rose steeply up the hillside. Climbing between maples, mountain laurel, and towering pines, we were overcome by a peacefulness we had never known anywhere else before. We felt we had found Our Spot, at last.

While sitting around the kitchen table negotiating with the owners and the agent, Max Simon suddenly announced how happy he and Becky were that this house would continue to be owned by Jewish people. With aged hands as shaky as his voice, he held up the package of deeds he'd been guarding for fifteen years— deeds that went back to the 1920s, their frayed and yellow pages naming all the Jews who had lived on this property.

Moved by this unexpected information and the poignancy with which it was conveyed, we felt like characters in a Bernard Malamud story. The idea of Jewish or not Jewish had never even occurred to us. Our only social concern had been how, as urbanized New Yorkers, we'd get along with rural New Englanders.

Still, Max's revelation evoked a warm feeling of collective identity between us and the Simons. Looking at them, we had a mystical feeling that this was meant to be. *Beschert*, as it is said in Yiddish. By stumbling into this particular house and community, we were living out some preordained sequence of events. Everyone, including the Christian agent, seemed to know we would fit in, be accepted, and get along here.

We were not the only ones so deeply enamored with this place. Over time, members of every family listed on the deeds Max had given us stopped by without advance notice. Bruce Kaplan was the first to knock on our door. Short, balding, and in his mid-forties, he fiddled with his glasses as he shyly explained who he was. Married and a bookkeeper, Bruce lived in a small house in a nearby town.

Exploring our rooms, he was astounded to see the alterations we had made in the old shed attached to the rear of the house. We had turned it into a spacious family room with a high ceiling and large windows that overlooked the back lawn and the ridge beyond it.

"This is where my mother kept the pickle barrel and the wood pile. We had no central heat. But," he added proudly, "our stoves kept the house toasty all winter long." He glued himself to the windows in a mournful reverie. "See out there, past the big maple? That's where my father planted a vegetable garden."

On entering the kitchen, Bruce recoiled. "Gee, this was our living room!" We told him about all the wallpaper we had to remove to redecorate the room, joking about how uncovering each layer was like conducting an archeological dig. But we didn't repeat what the old-timer helping us had said on finding the most garish design: "That one must be from the Kaplans. It looks just like them."

Lingering on the porch before departing, Bruce continued to reminisce. "I was only five years old during the flood of 1955. We were standing out here in the middle of the night watching the water rush down from the Silverbrook. Cars were floating all around. My mother's arms were loaded with blankets and pillows...we were waiting to be rescued by the Red Cross. But this house was on high ground, so we never got wet. We moved soon after that. It's funny," he said slowly, a wan smile on his face, "as frightened as I was then, I've always had such wonderful memories of living here." Finally tearing himself away and getting into the car, his sadness was so transparent we could read it: "Why had my father been foolish enough to sell this property?"

The next visitor was Harvey Blaustein, a tall, gray-haired lawyer who introduced himself with a dignified air. "We drove up from Long Island. This is my wife, Marsha."

"I don't understand him," she complained. "He won't let us take a vacation anywhere else. For years he's been talking about buying a piece of land. But all he does is *schlep* us from the Red Lion Inn just to look at this place. And where does it get him?" she asked, tugging at her designer jeans. "Every time he sees the changes people have made, he eats his heart out."

"It's enough, honey, he pleaded, following us into the house. As we passed the old brick oven behind the fireplace chimney, he exclaimed, "Oh, my God…I can smell my mother's bread baking! I can still see those loaves…round and shiny as she pulled them out on a long wooden paddle. And what a taste! We used to break off hot chunks and gobble them up before she even got them to the table."

"See what I mean?" his wife grumbled. Patting her bouffant hairdo, she addressed us condescendingly. "So how do you like living up here in the boonies? Not much to do, is there? I don't think I could take it."

Embarrassed by her comment, Mr. Blaustein seized her by the arm, thanked us abruptly, and steered her out the door.

Then came Bruce's sister, Debby, who owned a gift shop about thirty miles away. Like him, she was slight and bespectacled. Her eyes, while pleading innocence, flashed with covetous desire. She had come with her teenage daughter. Scrawny, pimpled, and dressed for a disco, the girl made no effort to hide her feelings of terminal ennui.

Grabbing her hand, Debby began to prowl the land with feral eagerness. Walking along the Clam River, she recounted how her father had maintained the farm. On the path leading into the woods, she paid homage to a dilapidated shed. "That's where the Indian...I mean the Native American...lived. He helped my Dad with all the heavy work. He slept out there in the dead of winter with only a small pot belly stove to keep him alive."

Sauntering around a graceful clump of apple trees, she told us tales of the tea parties she and her girlfriends had enjoyed beneath them. Her daughter, who plodded along as if towed by an iron leash, cried out, "If I hear her tell one more story about this place, I'm going to puke!" Grimacing, she whined on, "How she planted *this* and how they ate *that*...all their own fresh vegetables and eggs. And the great friends she had...how they played in the attic and dove into the swimming hole. It's too much...*really*!"

For several years, the "visitations" ceased. But one day Sue noticed a man and woman on the bridge in front of our house. They kept staring in our direction. Finally, full of trepidation, they moved toward our porch.

Opening the door, Sue called out, "Can I be of any help?"

"I *think* I'm in the right place," he began. "This is the old Polansky farm, isn't it? I'm his grandson, Steve Polansky…and this is my wife, Ann."

"I bet you'd love to look it over."

"How did you know?" he gasped.

"Well, we've had other visits from people who have lived here." Smiling to relax him, she continued. "We've heard a lot about your grandfather. He's quite famous in these parts. Wasn't he the one who had Russian Cossacks working the land?"

"I don't remember any Cossacks. But I'll never forget those winter and summer breaks I spent up here. They were the high points of my boyhood."

Having just retired from his position as an art professor at a college in Virginia, Steve told us he was doing the kind of "life review" advocated by gerontologists. He hadn't been in Sandisfield in over 50 years. Ann had never seen New England and was glad to accompany him on this journey to retrace his roots.

Avid to film everything in sight, Steve opened his camera and snapped one picture after another. "That's great what you've done in the attic, raising the roof along the stairway. Even as a kid there wasn't enough room for me to stand up in it. I remember how freezing it was sleeping up there in the winter."

After carefully descending the steep stairway to the living room, he confided, "I used to fly down those steps and warm up by the stove that was right about here. Sweeping his arm erratically along the wall where our couch stood, he seemed confused about where the stove had actually been. "My grandmother would wrap me up in a big feather comforter and hand me a steaming bowl of oatmeal."

He even took shots of the tiny half-basement, with its low ceiling and ancient hemlock beams encased in their original bark. Bumping his head while focusing the camera, he laughed good-naturedly. "Our children will love seeing this after all my talk about it."

These visits were vitally reassuring, given our discontent over the shortcomings we found in the house. The envious eyes of the former residents told us we were not crazy to have bought it. Walking them through the rooms and grounds, we were mesmerized by the rapt attention they gave to everything—once theirs—that now belonged to us. With each tour, we re-experienced the magnetic allure of Our Spot.

On the other hand, their acute nostalgia left us quite shaken. Here we were, knocking our brains out to imagine what new structural changes to make. And there they were, glorifying the quaint old woodshed we had modernized as a den; the tiny mullioned windows we had replaced with a six foot expanse of glass.

Assessing the changes they saw, these pilgrims to the past squinted into an invisible view finder. Bruce Kaplan recalled the red barn that stood where we keep a rock garden. Debby became distressed because she couldn't locate the strawberry patch her mother had cultivated. Steve Polansky pointed to what was once a meadow of wild flowers but had turned into a forest. And Harvey Blaustein appeared upset that the old brick oven was no longer in use.

It dawned on us that they were doing the same thing we were trying to do—erase the harsh realities of daily life and create a picture of perfect bliss. While we nurtured fantasies of bringing the imperfect present into an ideal future, they yearned to return to a time when they had felt the happiest.

Wanting to resurrect that idyllic interval in their lives, they came back here again and again. Perhaps, if they were lucky enough to choose the right day, the blurred negative in their minds would develop into a landscape so luminous as to dispel all the shadows of pain, doubt, and fear that advancing adulthood inevitably casts on everyone.

Eventually, we had the good fortune of finding an excellent contractor who was willing to take on the job of remodeling the house. But we were appalled to discover all the difficulties involved in removing the asbestos siding. It was necessary to get a special permit and find a company licensed to take off the shingles, which had to be wrapped properly and hauled all the way to a hazardous waste center in Pennsylvania.

Then, there were so many issues that had to be resolved. How should the porch be re-done? Screened in or left open? Should we use casement or double-hung windows in the kitchen? What color would best enhance the size and shape of the house?

Taking different positions on each of these questions, we were constantly arguing and screaming. Neither one of us was willing to yield to the other. During an especially wearing tiff, Sue asked for time-out. "God, are we ready to break up over a brand of paint?"

"Maybe if we could figure out what's really bothering us, we'd stop fighting," Irv said. "I think we're both being perfectionists. We want the house to make up for whatever defects we see in ourselves."

"The house *is* in public view. How can we avoid seeing it as a symbol of ourselves?"

"That's always been your trouble. You think the house and you are one."

"What about you, Mr. Big Shot? You bombarded these guys with a catalogue of specifications, right down to brass screws and double-dipped galvanized nails. Does that mean *you're* afraid of rotting away?"

"I guess it does. I must admit I've been trying to polish up my image."

"You bet. Any guy who wears a jade green parka and royal blue sweats is hoping to look more like a youthful peacock than an aging duck."

Lately, both of us had become extremely self-conscious about our appearance. We couldn't bear to watch the furrows being etched into our outer shells. Were we trying to give our domicile the transformation it was impossible to achieve for our own beings? Could we be nurturing the delusion that its attractiveness would effectively disguise—if not obliterate—our own debilitation? If we succeeded in imposing a whole "new look" on the house, would we be renewing our own lives and escaping the clutches of mortality?

"I think we're so uptight because this renovation is our final commitment to the house," Sue sighed.

"Yeah, our last hurrah."

"Every decision seems so irrevocable. Like we're closing off all our options. Once this work is done, we'll have no more changes to make. We'll be all set…"

"Exactly," Irv interrupted, "like in concrete. Or, if you prefer a more petrifying image, we'll be stiffs settled into our own tomb."

Scared witless by this prospect, we had become conspirators in a plot to forestall it, sabotaging the construction and postponing the completion of the job. Fortunately, we were able to end our crippling combat and make the decisions necessary for the carpenters to finish the work. In the middle of December, when they packed up their tools and drove away, we finally relaxed and allowed ourselves to enjoy the fruits of their labor.

On a warm day after the spring thaw, we circled the house to check for any damage the winter may have caused. Searching for sags in the gutters and chips in the paint, we marveled at how well the exterior had held up. Encouraged by this inspection, we returned to our lovely piazza and snuggled into a blanket of satisfaction, watching the sun play on the rippling river. Presently, a couple came strolling over the bridge, walking arm in arm.

"Hey," Irv whispered as they approached, "is that Debby Kaplan?"

"Hi," she said in a barely audible voice, ascending the porch steps. "I hope you don't mind me bothering you again."

"No, no," Sue assured her. "We're just sitting around."

Debby smiled with relief. "Thanks. I wanted to show my new husband where I lived as a child. But it's so different from the last time I was here."

"Yes," her husband said, shaking hands with us. "The house sure looks a lot better than I thought it would from Debby's description."

"Well," Irv smiled, "we've done a lot of work on it."

"I can see that."

"What you can't see are the asbestos shingles we had to tear off."

Sue took up the pitiful saga. "It would have been much cheaper if we had gotten rid of those awful things when we first came here. Back then, there were no environmental laws on how to deal with them."

Debby's husband nodded. "I know. It's a big problem now."

"And how!" Sue exclaimed. "After all that bother and expense, we were hoping the old clapboards could be salvaged. But they were too rotted," she rattled on, as if reliving a traumatic birth or surgical procedure. "It would have cost more to restore them than to buy these new ones."

Skimming the smooth gray surface of the boards, Debby's eyes dilated. "They look *very* good...and so does the white trim." Hesitating, she glanced toward her husband. "Is it O.K. if we walk around a little?"

"Fine, fine," we sang in two-part harmony.

After they were out of sight, Sue said, "I can't believe how attached she still is to this place. Who knows what she's gone through? Becoming a widow or getting divorced...and grief from her daughter, no doubt. But this guy seems nice."

"She must want to bring him into her fantasy land. Did you notice how zonked he was by the place?"

"It was hard to miss"

Irv chuckled. "I guess we turned an eyesore into a sight for sore eyes."

Laughing raucously, we almost failed to see the pair rounding the corner of the house. "Shh," Sue commanded, pasting up her grin.

Debby's eyes brimmed with longing. "That was great. And he enjoyed it as much as I did," she emphasized, looking at the husband she still had not introduced by name.

"Everything is so wonderful," he burst out, "...the river, the woods, the way the house sits on the land. I can see why she's so sentimental about this place."

With uncharacteristic humility, we had an urge to get down on our knees, kiss the ground, and thank Fate for bringing us here.

Awkward about what else to say, the couple seemed ready to leave. On their way to the road, Debby stopped and turned around with a pained expression on her face. "You know...my father was the one who put on those asbestos shingles. He thought they would make the house look prettier and easier to sell. We needed the money badly."

Dumbstruck, we waved goodbye. When they were far enough away, Irv mused, "How's that for human folly? Our trash was their treasure."

# USING IT WHILE
# LOSING IT

It was the day before Christmas in the Berkshires. The scene outside the picture window in our living room could have been a greeting card from Hallmark—if the artist had been God. Drifting in a low arc across a cobalt sky, the sun cast a golden sheen on the thick blanket of snow covering the tree-lined meadow. Picking up the light, prisms of frozen flakes shimmered like tiny rainbows on fire. Wherever we looked, tall stands of ash and maple were delicately powdered in white, their barren branches alive with the witchery of winter.

But the enchantment of these hills was not working for us today. Like a pair of silent Scrooges, we stared glumly at the splendor. Its utter serenity gave us no respite from our malaise.

Was loneliness the problem? Spending another holiday by ourselves with our children and grandchildren living so far away? Weren't all members of the dispersed American family supposed to get depressed during this festive season?

Perhaps it was the bitter aftertaste of our conversation during breakfast about the woeful state of the human condition. To us, it seemed to make the carols on the radio sound like raving absurdities. Only a Pollyannish simpleton could believe there was genuine peace anywhere on this troubled earth—or good will toward men.

Such bleak thoughts were not new to us. On many other occasions, we had faced the crushing prospect that people might let themselves follow the dinosaurs into extinction. Still, we had gone ahead and made each other happy. After all, wallowing in sadness would be of absolutely no use to anyone—including ourselves.

Irv let out a long and shuddering sigh. "What's the matter with us?

Actually, both of us knew the answer to his question. Yet we were refusing to admit that retirement had hit us as hard as it did other people. And we scoffed at any of the ways they typically use to soften the blow. Seeking to fulfill a long-suppressed desire for self-indulgence, some set sail on a Caribbean cruise, floating for weeks into exotic sunsets while a crew of attendants caters to their every whim. Others try to get similar pampering at Floridian resorts or spas in Arizona. If they want more adventure, they might go off on a trip to Alaska.

We would have none of these balms for our angst. No, we considered ourselves much too youthful and gifted for anything so obviously geriatric and unproductive. Besides, for years we had dreamed of becoming the completely creative couple—fulfilling the fantasy we harbored since the early days of our marriage. And we expected the atmosphere here to be as conducive to our creativity as it had been during our summers and sabbaticals.

A few weeks after our last lecture, we brought all our files and notes up to the house, ready to dig in with gusto to whatever we would write next. We were determined to make a productive workshop out of what we had always regarded as our "country retreat." But soon after unpacking, the shock of our unemployment exploded squarely between our tired eyeballs, spinning us into a vertigo of lassitude and disorientation.

The solitude of our setting also began to unnerve us. Irv lamented the loss of his status and role, which had beefed up his morale far more than he had been willing to acknowledge. Sue bemoaned our isolation, constantly harping on how essential it was to maintain social contacts. Mired in his funk, Irv would usually snarl, "Who needs them?" But whenever he did agree to her suggestion for a dinner party, she sank into a quicksand of lethargy, powerless to decide who to have and what to serve.

We had always taken pride in being exceptionally self-motivated and bristled at the thought of booking ourselves up for months in advance with tickets to Tanglewood or Jacobs Pillow. Who knew what mood we'd be in on the dates we'd reserved?

Yet since retiring, we had established rigid routines to avoid facing the ambiguity of our future. Regardless of whether or not we were hungry, we began our three meals at exactly the same hours each day and went to bed at 9:30 P.M. with equal precision. Even our physiological functioning had become synchronized. If one of us suffered heartburn after too rich a meal, so did the other. At night, we got up to pee at three. And our morning coffee had the same expulsive effect on both of us.

Periodically, we went berserk from feeling locked into this fixed pattern. Yet we continued to mope around in a dispirited haze of dread. How quickly would we lose our remaining strength? What ailments might strike us?

Would death show up at the door in the morning and demand our bones for breakfast?

"Let's stop feeling so sorry for ourselves," Sue screamed, jumping up from her swivel rocker. "C'mon," she insisted, "we promised to visit Larry. He's been in the nursing home for months. Remember how many years he watched over our house? And all the work he did for us?"

"You couldn't choose a more uplifting activity, could you?"

"Oh quit it!" Stomping into the kitchen, she picked up a box of cookies. "A brisk walk in the fresh air will do us good."

Bundled in hooded parkas, we crept down the icy steps of our front porch and trudged onto the roadway. Our boots crunched out rhythmic squeals against the tightly packed snow. With our arms linked, we lurched from side to side like figure skaters performing a drunken *pas de deux*. Bending our heads to fight the frosty sting of the wind, we could barely see where we were going.

The road meandered along the bottom of our river valley—far from the mainstream and the fast track. In fact, the railroad barons of the middle 1800s ran their tracks many miles to the east of us. After having been the Boomtown of the Berkshires during the industrial revolution, our town slid into laid-back seclusion. Only relics of its former bustle can be seen today—the crumbling rock foundations that stood beneath the busy mills on the river banks. T-shirts sold at summer fairs call it the ghost town of the Berkshires, or ask, "Where the h— is Sandisfield?

Located in the southeast corner of the county, the town is as big as Manhattan in square miles. But the permanent population is only about 900. Sue takes perverse glee in saying that we're living on the "Lower East Side," when meeting other New Yorkers, who, like ourselves, don't know exactly why they ended up here— except that you can get more for your money than in more fashionable parts of the Berkshires.

Our town offers remarkable scenic beauty but none of the tourist attractions found in Lenox or Stockbridge. Sandisfield has only one enduring claim to cultural fame—the classic Christmas carol composed here over a century ago by the Reverend Edmund H. Sears: *It Came Upon a Midnight Clear*.

As we plodded along, our frustrations continued to gnaw at us. "I don't know why we've been complaining so much about being retired. For years we bitched about having to conform to an academic mold," Irv ranted, sending spurts of steam into the air. "All those rigid rules and schedules were stifling."

"But we're free at last," Sue shouted into the wind, "free to call our own shots and set our own pace."

"So how come we haven't been using our freedom?"

"Well…didn't Janice Joplin say that freedom's just another word for nothing left to lose?"

"What's her old lyric got to do with us now?" Irv snapped.

"Maybe that's what's bothering us," she retorted. "We can't use our freedom because we're still trying so hard to hold on to things we've already lost."

Her comment was right on the mark. Despite our dissatisfactions, we couldn't deny the kicks we had gotten out of teaching together. It thrilled us to see the impact we made on our students. And being accepted by college kids made us feel almost as young as them.

Irv sped forward. "Let's be really honest. We became addicted to getting so many pellets of adulation. Those are the goodies we miss so much…and neither one of us wants to admit they're gone forever."

Sue rushed to keep up. "And we certainly loved it when reviewers praised our books. We don't want to lose out on those accomplishments, either."

"That's why we're so upset about giving up our old routine. It's given us whatever success we've had. We're terrified of opening ourselves to something new."

"Maybe we should just ease up and lie fallow," she suggested, "until something really inspires us."

"We both might be six feet under by the time that happens."

The sight of the nursing home brought our conversation to a jarring end. Its low-slung brick facade was the embodiment of institutional dreariness. We tried to enter with smiling faces but failed.

The overheated lobby was empty. Partly blinded by the condensation on our glasses, we blinked at the Kmart decor surrounding us. Scallops of frayed tinsel draped the walls. A pine tree in the center of the room was strung with colored lights, which glittered on and off erratically. A large fluorescent fixture on the ceiling cast a ghastly glow over the joyless scene. The air reeked with a nauseating mix of urine and antiseptics.

"Maybe this was a mistake," Sue whispered tremulously.

Before Irv could spew out a snide rejoinder, an attendant came out of a doorway. Tall, blonde, and bouncy, she seemed to have just stepped out of a square dance. Had she been dipping into a bottle of Christmas "cheer" hidden in a utility room? "Hi! My name is Karen. What can I do for you?"

"We're here to visit Larry," Irv said.

Pointing toward his room, Karen reviewed Larry's condition. He eats and sleeps well, takes his medication, and gives the staff no trouble. Since he has difficulty walking, he stays in his room a lot. But he never whines about anything.

Thanking her profusely, we pulled off our coats and headed down the long corridor. Several doors were ajar and we heard some wheezing coughs. "We better take extra Vitamin C when we get home," Irv mumbled.

Larry's door was wide open. We went in cautiously and found him stretched out in bed. Gaunt and withered, with his eyes closed and mouth agape, he looked like a corpse waiting to be carried off to a funeral parlor.

Clearing his throat vigorously, Irv called out, "Hey, Larry, look who's here."

He half-lifted one eye, then the other. "Hello," he croaked.

"Karen tells us you're doing fine," Sue gushed. "here's some cookies…vanilla…the soft kind you like."

Larry allowed himself the toothless semblance of a smile. "Yes, they treat me good. Food ain't too bad. Thanks, I'll have one of those." He sat up with surprising animation. "Only one thing is…" Munching, he tapped a gnarled finger on the side of his bald head. "There's a lot of kooks here. One of them yells all the time. And some won't even say a word. Like that guy over there," he cackled, turning his bleary blue eyes toward the far side of the room.

Startled, we stared across an empty bed and saw a man seated in a chair. Hunched over a book, he was reading with an attention so focused it excluded everything else in the world—including our presence.

"Reads all the time, he does," Larry said, loud enough for his roommate to hear. "Never wants to talk. Used to be a professor. Ah, what the heck, he's O.K. Better than the screamer."

Irv couldn't contain himself. "A professor?" he hissed, like a balloon rapidly losing air. "Sue, a professor!"

She shook her head incredulously and murmured, "Maybe Larry's losing it."

By now, Larry had slumped under the covers and shut his eyes again. We took this to mean he'd had quite enough socializing. But we felt compelled to stay a few minutes longer, immobilized by an eerie fascination with "the professor." He was neatly dressed in a tan cardigan and tweed slacks. His salt-and-pepper hair was well combed and his oval face clean-shaven. Peering at the pages through his steel-rimmed glasses, he could have passed for normal in the reference room of any university library.

Irv prodded an elbow into Sue's arm, his patented gesture for us to terminate a visit. She arose at once, equally eager to leave the room.

"Bye, Larry,"

"Bye," Irv echoed.

Larry had already gone bye-bye into the Land of Nod. His rasping snores followed us for some distance on our return to the lobby.

Near the entrance, Karen asked, "Good visit?"

"Oh, yeah," Irv lied shamelessly. "Larry's in great shape. He's quite a guy...but his roommate...he stumped us."

"Is he really a professor?" Sue blurted out, impatient with Irv's equivocation.

"Oh, yes," Karen replied emphatically. "That is, he was once. A professor of literature at an Ivy League college."

"Oh!" Irv exclaimed. "Now I understand why he had so many books on his table."

"Does he actually read them?" Sue persisted.

"He sure does. Cover to cover. But he can't remember what he takes in. So he reads them over and over and over."

"I was a professor, too," Irv confessed warily, as if this fact alone might be sufficient to qualify him for admission to Karen's establishment.

"Yes, and I was a co-teacher with him…in psychology at NYU," Sue chimed in, not wanting to be left out. "How did Larry's roommate get here?"

Karen became slightly officious. "Well, you understand, I can't give out confidential information. All I can say is he's one of the men transferred here from a veterans' hospital."

Of course, we silently said to ourselves. He's one of the mental patients Larry mentioned.

A gust of wind showered us with a glaze of snow as we started the daunting trek back to our house. The crystal air was a welcome head-cleanser. But we couldn't shake off our preoccupation with the professor. Puffing and panting, we exchanged conjectures about his situation. We had heard rumors that many of the residents in the nursing home were ex-alcoholics. Most likely, his memory loss came from years of heavy drinking. His incessant reading also pointed to the perseveration often found among people with brain damage.

At the driveway to our house, we realized why we had been so rattled by him. Naturally, we identified with his plight. We had frequently envisioned the calamity of winding up in a nursing home ourselves. And we devoutly hoped that we would somehow be spared from such an appalling finale to our lives. But what bothered us most was how his repetitive behavior reflected our own hang-up. Weren't we in the same bag—going round and round and round on which project to do? Endlessly chewing over exactly the same pros, cons, ifs, ands, and buts. Yet making no choices and taking no action. On entering the kitchen, a common panic seized us: Could *our* brains be corroding from the sheer effects of aging?

"O.K.," Irv announced, like a military leader preparing troops for a dangerous mission. "This is it. We've got to go over the line of our waffling. I think we're in a little better shape than our colleague in the nursing home! But who knows how much longer our combined brain power will last?"

"I know, I know. Whatever we do takes us longer. And we forget more things. But we don't have to go on acting like a pair of impotent slugs."

"Janice Joplin was pushing a bunch of hippie hype. People always have something left to lose…they're never free from the possibility of wasting the precious time of their lives," Irv said. "How about the Grateful Dead's version of Joplin's line?" Using his fist as a microphone, he mimicked Jerry Garcia's twang. "Freedom's just another word for nothing left to *do*."

"We've sure been doing a lot of nothing lately. But where has that gotten us?"

"Not too far. We feel worse doing nothing than we did when we were breaking our humps to create something we liked. Now we don't seem to feel anything is worth doing."

"That's our sour grapes. If we can't surpass...or at least equal...what we've done before, we don't want to do anything."

"And if we don't do anything, nobody can detect our shortcomings. Can they?" Irv asked, quickly adding, "And neither can we."

"But we've still got a lot in us that we want to express." Sue insisted. "Maybe what we've been trying to say is that freedom's just another word for doing what we *want* to do...within the limits of what we *can* do."

"Well, there's no other way to prove we can do something than by doing it!"

Beaming at each other, we shed our Eskimo outfits. Sue clicked on the oven and put in the lasagne she had prepared earlier for dinner.

"Wow, I sure lucked out by marrying you. What efficiency!"

"I'm looking forward to being as efficient with our writing again. I miss the marvelous feeling of intimacy we get when we work well together. All that mental interpenetration. It's almost like making love."

Irv squeezed her shoulders. "If you're so hot to trot, let's skip dinner and go to it."

"No way. At our age, we need all the sustenance we can get before taking that kind of plunge."

We floated through dinner enclosed in a magical bubble of contentment. Relishing our glasses of burgundy, we pulled our chairs in front of the fireplace. The crackling logs accompanied the soothing sounds of a Baroque guitar solo emanating from the CD player our children gave us for our last anniversary. Soon, our longing for sensual contact became too urgent to resist. Wordlessly, we got up, closed the fireplace screen and headed for our bedroom.

Sue undressed leisurely. Dawdling as she put away her clothes, she savored the delicious sensations that had begun to course through her body.

Returning from the shower, Irv was lit up with anticipation. "O.K., it's all yours." Picking up a magazine, he tried to distract himself until she got back. But when he heard her moving around in the bathroom after the water stopped running, his patience ran out. "I bet you're doing your goddamn mirror number," he shouted, "checking out your daily changes."

Sue reappeared before he could finish his tirade.

"Find any more wrinkles? Don't worry. I'll never stop loving you, my sweet little filly."

"Well, at least you didn't call me your old gray mare," she laughed, joining Irv in bed. Here, let me hold you a little bit."

"A little bit? Nothing doing. You know with me it's either all or nothing!"

"What an extremist! But that's what I've always loved about you."

Through the bedroom windows, we caught a glimpse of the sunset, its waning tints of mauve infusing the fleecy clouds sailing over the ridge. Fanning out beneath the clouds, luminous bands of blue and green melted into the darkening hills. Melting, melting—just as our minds were sweeping away, our bodies dissolving into each other.

At last, we let go. Letting ourselves experience every wave of ecstasy we had learned to unleash. Knowing just the right spots to touch. Tenderly stroking, kissing. That's it, just there! Once more. Yes, yes…Every part of us pulsating as our excitement mounted to an irrepressible crescendo. Going limp, our arms spread out at our sides. Suddenly we embraced again, sating the last twinges of our desire.

Fantastic, wasn't it, Irv?"

"And how! We've been feeling dead for so long, we couldn't make love anything like this."

Sue gazed out at the sky. "I love being in bed with you at this time of day, watching it turn from dusk to dark.

"I guess we finally had a great Christmas Eve. Of course, we didn't wait for midnight to celebrate. But we came upon a twilight clear!"

# UP AND DOWN THE SLIPPERY SLOPE

In remodeling the exterior of our house, the workmen had to strip off the original layer of rotted clapboards. Although this slow unveiling was not as titillating as a burlesque act, it aroused our apprehensive curiosity. What kind of body would we find beneath the drab and tattered garments the old girl had worn for so long?

Stark naked, the walls gave us instant relief. The wide planks of hemlock, more than an inch thick, showed no signs of deterioration after two centuries. However, nothing but emptiness stood between those boards and the plaster and lath lining of the rooms inside.

Our contractor advised us to fill the space with cellulose insulation. It would be easy to drill holes through the exposed walls and pump in the stuff. He also recommended insulating the large area between the ceiling of our living room and the unheated attic above it. To do that, it would be necessary to go up there and drill holes through the wooden floor. So we had to clear out any clutter that might get in the way.

With leaden feet, we shuffled along the hallway adjoining the living room and pulled down the folding stairway. Shakily, we climbed into the quaintest room in the house. This musty chamber had always seduced us into the dreaminess of a fairy tale. We had often fantasized how to convert it into an exquisite hideaway for writing and painting.

Invariably, however, we awakened to the fact that the space was too small to warrant such expense. Following the tradition followed by our predecessors, we kept using it as a storage bin. Now, we had to take out almost everything in sight.

Intimidated by the scope of our task, we lapsed into a daze of hesitation. How could we have accumulated so much junk and debris? Aluminum storm windows, pocked and pitted, leaned against the nearest wall. A jagged trail of broken panes twinkled on the filthy carpet lining the dusty floor. Several of Sue's old paintings and portfolios of drawings were crammed under adjacent eaves. Beyond this abandoned art collection were the shelves and bricks of a makeshift bookcase from the leaner days of our arrival in the Berkshires. In the distance, a blanket of cobwebs spread over a jumble of discarded furniture. Battered tables and chairs—missing legs or arms—clung together like amputees huddling for mutual support.

What oppressed us most were the cardboard boxes strewn around the room. Boxes, boxes, boxes of every size and shape, boxing us into a long-deferred confrontation with our lunacy. Many were laden with "important papers": the early medical histories of our adult children; tax records and canceled checks dating back to the 1960s; faded class notes from our college days. Some contained old clothing never given, as planned, to the Goodwill. Others held defunct kitchen appliances never repaired, as intended. A few bulged with scraps of leftover fabric from sewing projects Sue had finished decades ago.

However, we were amazed to find that most of the boxes were empty, tightly stacked inside one another, like Russian nesting dolls. After peering into the third stack, Irv blew his own. "This is perfect kindling for a big burst of spontaneous combustion in a really hot summer. But you *desperately* need these goddamn boxes!"

Kicking the closest carton, Sue growled, "What about you? You just *love* to throw things out. Remember when you chucked all those good shirts and sheets into the compactor at the dump?"

"Well, you were the one who put them in black trash bags. You were too cheap to buy a proper laundry basket."

"But you don't appreciate the value of anything. If it weren't for me, we wouldn't have any of the lovely things we inherited from our parents."

"The main thing you inherited was your father's instinct for hoarding. And since we're throwing up the past, remember that suitcase full of empty jewelry boxes we found in his closet after he died?"

"O.K., O.K. He was a little fiendish about containers. But he needed them for mailing merchandise to his customers."

"So who are your customers?" Irv sneered.

"You know we need boxes to send out presents. And didn't those cartons from the stereo and TV come in handy when we made the move up here?"

"Naturally, we're going to move somewhere else any day now."

"Look, let's make a deal," Sue implored. "We'll get rid of most of them. But we'll keep a few outside in the shed."

On this note of compromise, we started hauling away whatever was disposable. Then we tackled the onerous chore of making room downstairs for the numerous items we decided to save. After a weekend of hard labor, we had the mess straightened out. On Sunday night, Sue went up to the attic again to make sure the decks were cleared.

The next morning, the insulation man showed up with an assistant to help drill the holes and monitor the pressure of the powerful machine they brought to pump in the cellulose. After leading them to the attic, we went into our nearby study. But the wild whirring of the electric drills made it hard to concentrate on our work.

Suddenly, the din ceased and the assistant let out a piercing shriek. Thinking he had injured himself, we bolted from our chairs. But we were brought to a halt by a fit of maniacal laughter.

Sue gasped. "What the hell is going on? What can be *that* funny? My God…maybe I left one of my nude paintings up there."

Before Irv had a chance to answer, we heard another tumultuous roar from the assistant. "I can't believe it! How could this be? These are *my* skis…the first pair I ever owned! Look…they have my name on them in gold letters…Vincent Franco. This is far out!"

Frowning at Sue, Irv whispered, "I thought we put those old skis out in the shed."

"You're thinking of the poles. We've been using them to slog through the snow. I saw the skis up there last night behind one of the rafters. But I…"

Vince rushed into our study, his arms cradling the skis. Patting them tenderly, he grinned and shook his head. "I haven't seen these babies for almost twenty years. How did you get them?"

"They belonged to our son," Sue explained. "Maybe he bought them from you! He lived here around that time."

"I don't know...I can't remember who I sold them to."

"They probably passed through a few other hands before our son got them," Irv suggested.

"Yeah," Sue added. "Do you know Dan Green or Jack Conklin? He was very close to them." For a few seconds, she drifted off, recalling the days when the house was constantly filled with our kids' friends—cooking, playing music, and dancing before crashing out on the floor in their sleeping bags. "Or maybe it was Joe Levitt."

"Sorry, nothing rings a bell." Vince raised the skis triumphantly over his head. "Quite a trophy to hang over the mantle!"

Of course, it would be the right thing to give him the skis. We certainly had no use for them. Besides, they were antiques compared with the sleek runners in vogue today.

Still, neither of us acknowledged Vince's implicit request. In the past, we would have responded with immediate generosity, happy to be linked to him in some "cosmic" chain of connection. Our retentiveness felt strangely unexpected and out of character. Had aging made us too miserly to part with even the most worthless of objects?

"Right," Sue muttered belatedly, embarrassed by our obvious reluctance to offer him the skis. "Our son will get a tremendous kick hearing about this."

"I'm sure he will," Vince mumbled sadly. No longer smiling, he looked tired. Traces of his forty-something years—the creases in his brow and along the sides of his mouth—were accentuated by his deflation, betraying the aura of youthful bravado he tried to exude. Trudging upstairs to resume his work, Vince said, "If he doesn't want the skis, I'd be glad to take them off your hands."

Back in our study, we withdrew from each other. Irv was eager to continue writing. Sue begged off, telling him she wanted to finish reading an article. Actually, she needed to calm down from the disturbing encounter with Vince. The printed words swam before her eyes like tiny minnows as she fished for understanding in the ruffled waters of her mind.

What's gotten into me? Why hadn't I taken those skis out to the shed? Could I have wanted them for myself? I never even learned to stand up on skis. But how I wished to go skiing when I was in elementary school—like the rich kids. Their parents had country homes and took them to Europe on winter vacations. Stuck in Brooklyn, I had to be satisfied with ice skating on the Prospect Park Lake. Oh, I *was* great at it. I loved to bend low and cross one leg over the other as I swiftly cut around corners. I felt so light and graceful gliding over the surface of the ice. My body seemed weightless and my cheeks flushed with the excitement of seeing myself as Sonja Henie, the most famous figure skater of that era.

But to ski—that was my ultimate dream. I could easily conjure up the thrill of flying down a particularly steep trail, my torso and limbs perfectly aligned, my ski poles held at just the right angle, my hair flowing freely in the wind, the feathery swish of snow blowing up around me as I maneuvered to end the dazzling run with a flourish. In my fantasies, I never faltered or fell. Conquering the loftiest peaks of the Alps, I was a soaring superwoman in my favorite country, not a little girl whose Switzerland was a flat map in a geography book.

"Could you put that article down for a few minutes?" Irv asked. "I need your help here."

Sue dropped the magazine. "I couldn't read. I was thinking about Vince's skis…and what they might mean to me."

"So what illuminations did you come up with?"

"Don't get nasty, Irv. My thoughts were just as applicable to you."

"Like what?"

"Like my frustration about never doing some of the things that appealed to me so much. I went back to when I was a girl pining for a pair of skis…"

"What does that have to do with me? I never had the slightest desire to go skiing."

"You just wanted different things. But you had the same regrets about not doing them. What about your boyish dreams of being on the Davis Cup team?"

"Hey, I swung a wicked racket for a kid of ten. So...the skis represent the unfulfilled aspirations of childhood?"

"Now you're getting it. They're symbols of the youth we don't want to lose...even though it's long gone."

"I guess they also remind us of when our children were still young." Irv mused. "Having them around made us feel so vital and needed."

"We had a hard time letting go of them, too."

"So we want to be younger than we are...and we wish we had accomplished everything we ever dreamt of doing. Big Deal! What else is new?"

"What's new," Sue smiled, "is that I get the shakes just watching people sitting in ski lifts."

"Me, too. But we have to look at them whenever we pass Butternut Basin in the winter. Imagine how scared we'd be going up the mountainside in one of those chairs."

"You think we've lost our daring?"

"We sure have," Irv acknowledged, "when it comes to risking our necks."

"When we were young, we thought it was great fun to master the forces of nature."

"That's why you were so thrilled by the idea of skiing...defying gravity and turning a dangerous descent into a spectacular feat of athletic skill."

"And we could always be successful in our imagination."

"So I made myself a tennis star while you became a skating champion."

"Now, the only sport *you* participate in is squirting powder on your athlete's foot."

Sue's jest was a feeble attempt to lighten the truth. We were being rapidly dragged down the slippery slope of existence. If we were very lucky, we might have another twenty years—more or less—on this slide. But there was no denying its gathering speed.

Lost in our personal pre-occupations, we reacted numbly as the workers finished insulating the house and left. Vince went home empty-handed. But the youthful memories ticked off by the incident continued to rub our noses in the fragility of our condition.

We had no more distractions to keep from getting totally involved in our writing. Still, something prevented us from starting. Could it be our fear of revealing hidden aspects of ourselves? But what was the worst that could happen? Surely, nothing as terrible as being smothered by blocked energy.

Having lost touch with our founts of inspiration, we struggled like parched nomads to open up the pipeline to our recalcitrant muse. One of us picked up a pen; the other pecked away at a keyboard. Probing furiously with these tools, we strove to dig up the words that would dislodge our inner impediments. As these efforts failed, we threw ourselves into any activity except writing, hoping the change would stimulate a breakthrough.

Actually, we had no choice but to wait until a fresh "shipment" welled up from some mysterious source within us. Regardless of what we did while waiting, we were keenly aware of being in the grip of a force that was as powerful as gravity is for skiers. To keep our balance, we had to rely on blind faith and unremitting perseverance. Otherwise, we would have fallen into a state of despondency severe enough to make us quit altogether.

When our "shipments" finally arrived, we were rewarded for riding out this excruciating interval of incubation. The gap between the emergence of our ideas and the act of putting them into words was imperceptible. Enchanted by this spontaneity, we experienced an incomparable rush in guiding the articulation of our thoughts—like skiers who artfully modulate their acceleration on an unexpected drop in their path.

Our collaboration began to give us an excitement equivalent to skiing. Of course, our adventures occurred in the quiet of our study. Blank sheets of paper were our snowy slopes. Pen and computer were our pair of skis. The hazards we faced were psychological, not physical. But when we zipped into the climax of our outpourings, we felt the same transcendent elation as any skiers who successfully brave the foothills of the Mattahorn.

Convinced that our indoor activity was as exhilarating as any outdoor sport, we could give up the illusion of being youthful daredevils. At our age, risking our sanity was sufficient to proving our prowess. We didn't have to incur the risk of breaking our legs, too.

Toward the end of winter, with two feet of snow still on the ground, a pickup truck appeared in our driveway. Vincent hopped out and headed for our door.

Sue greeted him delightedly. "I bet I know what you've come for. We want you to have the skis."

"Are you sure? I was passing through these parts on the way to a job and I just had to stop by to see if I could get them."

"We're certainly glad you did. Irv," she called, "look who's here. It's Vince!"

"What d'ya know!" Irv responded from the living room. "Wait a minute. I'll go up to the attic."

Alone in the kitchen with Vince, Sue groped for a topic of conversation. "How do you like this weather? We've had some pretty heavy snow. Of course, it's very good for skiing. Do you do much of it?"

"Not like I used to," he admitted regretfully. On seeing Irv return with the skis, Vince recovered his zest. "Gee, this is great!" he exclaimed, seizing them as if fearful we might have a change of heart.

"You know," Irv said, "Our son couldn't get over how you found the skis. He didn't remember the guy he got them from, either."

After Vince thanked us and drove away, Sue quipped, "Ten to one, they'll wind up going from his mantle to *his* attic."

"Well, if he needs them to feel he's still at the top of his form…so be it."

# LOOKING FOR
# DR. RIGHT

In the year since our retirement, neither of us had become ill. Yet that very fact was getting to us. How long would our luck hold out? Since we were spending so much time at our house, it hit us that it would be a good idea to have a doctor in the vicinity in case of any emergency. But how could we find an internist worthy of our trust?

Both of us sensed our unwillingness to resolve this issue was laden with irrationality—with roiling undercurrents of resistance we would have to swim through before reaching the calm shores of consensus. Equally agitated by the fear underlying our vacillation, we showed it in different ways. Doing his typical number, Irv retreated into a shell of silence, pretending that nothing bothered him. Playing my complementary role in our division of defensive behavior, I became fiendishly obsessed with the idea of finding a doctor.

"I don't know why you've started to worry so much," Irv grumbled.

"What do you mean…I'm worrying? What about you? You're not kidding me. You're as scared as I am. You're just trying to make me the designated patient."

"Well, you're the one who's complained about gaining so much weight. Don't forget, there's a history of diabetes and heart trouble in your family."

"Do you have to rub it in? I know I've been letting myself go since we stopped teaching. And I haven't had a thorough checkup in years. But what about my annual trips to the gynecologist? I'd like to see how you'd react to having someone probe your private parts!"

"Oh, so you're blaming me because I'm *only* a man? Is it my fault? I didn't invent female anatomy. It just happens that women need special care for their equipment."

"Men have their own vulnerabilities. What about your prostate? You won't even discuss the possibility of getting that new blood test. Every time I mention it, you flare up and change the subject. And colon cancer doesn't have any sexual preference."

"You're trying to squirm out of your own problem. I had a complete physical four years ago and got a clean bill of health."

"Yeah, it's normal to get up so often every night to piss."

"Stop exaggerating. Lots of men my age do that."

"I'm tired of always being the one who has to go to a doctor. Even before our wedding, I had to get a diaphragm. Then there were pap smears. When I switched to the pill, I had to worry about my fibroid growing from the size of a lemon to a grapefruit. Thank goodness, it shriveled to a pea after menopause. By that time, I had to start with mammograms…having my tits shoved into an x-ray machine. How would you like to have your balls jammed into a vice and then wait to see if they needed to be lopped off?"

"Please, that's enough! God, what you women go through!"

"I can't believe *you* agree with that. But it's true. And it hasn't been fun for me to change doctors every time we've moved."

"It's probably just as well you were forced to find a gynecologist in the Berkshires. Otherwise, you might still be looking for one…plus an internist."

It started during our winter break the year before we retired. There it was on the toilet tissue I used after urinating one morning. An insignificant spot of blood, which instantly became highly significant for me. Not bright read or crimson. Just a tannish-rose streak lightly smeared on the clear white background. The color got more intense as I wiped again. Damn it, another bladder infection! I had one a few years ago. Only now, the painful burning was missing.

I gently grazed my urethra with a fresh piece of paper. The staining disappeared. Where the hell had it come from? Twisting backwards, I touched the area near my anus. Sometimes, little pink polka dots gave me telltale signs of irritated hemorrhoids. Today, there were none.

Then I placed the tissue against the middle and pushed it up into my vagina. Ridiculous. This couldn't possibly be the source. I hadn't bled there in over a dozen years. Not since that one time a year after my last period. The doctor had immediately scheduled me for a D&C. Any bleeding after menopause could be dangerous, he had said. But the procedure showed there was nothing to worry about.

When I pulled my hand away and saw new smudges of blood, I cringed. Testing again, I got the same results. This was definitely the right orifice.

It was probably another false alarm. It could wait until we got back to New York. I had an appointment for my annual visit to the gynecologist at the end of January. But what about our neighbor down the road? Starting with exactly the same symptom, she had died from ovarian cancer within a few months. And she was quite a bit younger than me.

Shuddering, I stared out at the mounds of snow piled up to the sill of our bathroom window. Lilac branches, iced into a filigree of stiff lace, scratched menacingly against the frosted panes. Obviously, I couldn't ignore the bleeding. Rushing back to the city on hazardous roads wouldn't be smart, either. So I phoned my doctor in Manhattan to see what he advised. It could be something minor or something serious, he said. I should waste no time in getting it checked out up here.

Then I called a friend who recommended Dr. Stein. He delivered all three of her children and she'd been in his care for fifteen years. She said he was competent, understanding, and witty—the kind of person I'd find sympatico. He was also a transplant from New York.

I still didn't feel completely reassured. I had always been nervous before seeing a gynecologist. For days before my appointments, I'd rehearse what I wanted to say. Sometimes, I'd even write out my questions. While waiting naked and shivering on the examining table for the doctor to rush in and "do his thing," I'd furtively bone up on my list—like a coed sneaking crib notes into a biology exam. Often, the doctors were more reluctant to answer my questions than I was to ask them. Their replies tended to be perfunctory, as if they were being unduly delayed from having similarly hurried encounters with the women penned into all the other cubicles in the office.

After a quick look, Dr. Stein allayed my fears. "Don't worry, you're no Gilda Radnor. We used to call what you have a senile vagina," he said. "Now that we're more sensitive to women's feelings, we've changed the diagnosis to atrophic vaginitis."

My friend's description was very accurate. This guy was some joker! But humor was just the medicine I needed.

Going from jester to father figure, he looked at me with genuine empathy. "None of us is getting any younger. It's natural at your age. There's nothing wrong that a topical application of estrogen cream can't cure. You'll need to use it as long as you want to keep on having intercourse." Opening a cabinet on the wall, he gave me a handful of samples. "This should do until you get back to New York and see what your doctor there thinks."

As we exchanged impressions about how life in the Berkshires compared to the Big Apple, I let him know that Irv and I taught a course on human sexuality at NYU. After some hesitation, I also told him that we'd soon be retiring and spending a lot of time up here. He said he'd be glad to take me on as a regular patient.

Returning to the waiting room, I gave Irv a comforting smile. I didn't have cancer! And I had found a gynecologist I liked.

On the way home, my mood took a nose dive. Was I joining the ranks of the estrogen junkies? Luckily, I didn't have to wear a patch. Yet the cream I had to use might be as much a killer as a cure. What a double bind! There was no cancer corroding my ovaries. But the only medication available for my vagina put me at risk for cancer of the uterus. Contrary to the stereotyped notion, I never experienced menopause as a big deal. Although I had some hot flashes, I was liberated from the daily discipline of remembering to take my birth control pills. Since our adult children were no longer living at home, we had all the privacy we desired. Instead of spoiling our sexual pleasure, menopause actually enhanced it.

Now, at the age of only sixty-three, I had a "senile vagina." It was kind of the doctor to qualify his terminology. But why did he use it in the first place? Perhaps his charming bedside manner was a camouflage for his true feelings. I was an old hag like all the others he was obliged to treat. If my vagina was senile, could my brain be far behind?

I hadn't been totally honest, either. Eager to impress him as a vivacious sex pot, I didn't mention how difficult it had become for me to get lubricated. When I felt aroused, it took a lot of time and clitoral stimulation for my fluids to flow. The more tense I became about getting wet, the drier I got.

As a result, Irv and I had trouble coordinating our moves. Fearing that he would lose his erection, I sometimes urged him to go ahead before I was ready. When he did, he knew I wasn't moist enough. Both of us paid dearly for those charades. I had pain, frustration, and now bleeding. He experienced a mixture of confusion and guilt.

My new "estrogen fix" was nothing short of a miracle. In a few months my vaginal tissues were soft and supple. After I returned to my normal level of lubrication, our intercourse became as mutually satisfying as it was before my "dry spell."

When my diagnosis and remedy were confirmed by my gynecologist in New York, I decided to make a permanent change to Dr. Stein. The following January, six months after our retirement, I went to him for my regular checkup. He was pleased by the effect of the estrogen. According to him, very little of the hormone was being absorbed into my system. I could stop worrying about negative side effects. Everything else was normal. He did comment on my increased weight and asked if I had an internist. Embarrassed, I confessed that I hadn't seen one in over twelve years.

"At your age, that's a bit like playing Russian Roulette...don't you think?" He gave me a card with the names of two people that he said were excellent.

I thanked him profusely and put the card in my wallet. As soon as I left the office, the idea of calling one of the internists seemed to lose its urgency. I had attended to my scariest problem. The rest of my body could wait until I had a good reason to deal with it.

Shortly afterward, winter hit the Berkshires with a blast. Rarely able to travel to our studio in New York, the weather kept us inside much of the time. The full force of my personal reaction to our retirement was starting to hit me. True, I had agreed with Irv about wanting more freedom to do creative work. But the lack of social feedback was more burdensome than I had bargained for.

Knowing I could no longer get the admiration of students, I had begun to neglect my appearance. What difference did it make how I dressed? Who would see me if I went around in rags? Did it matter how disheveled I looked? Even if I got heavy as a horse, nobody would think any less of me. Whenever I caught a glimpse of myself in the full-length mirror, I glared at my bulging stomach and double chin. Disgusted, I'd run into the kitchen and eat a cookie to lift my sagging spirits.

Frozen into depression, my emotions didn't thaw with the arrival of spring. I couldn't resonate with the renewal of life all around us. The golden crocuses popping up warmed me no more than the dregs of snow surrounding them.

Recently, a strange symptom added to my gloom. Every night, I would wake up two or three times with my bowels in an uproar. This was a dramatic change from my habitual pattern of defecating once a day after morning coffee. Could it be due to an overdose of Vitamin C? Or were these "runs" expressing an attempt to run from myself?

My body was sending me an unequivocal message: Get a doctor. Following up on the names Dr. Stein had recommended, I found that neither of them could add any new patients to their caseloads. Next, I tried a couple of internists suggested by friends. They were also filled to capacity. Had somebody put a hex on me? Was there any decent physician left for me to try?

Frenetically, I scurried around quizzing all the people I respected about the internists they used. I was referred to two doctors who could see me. But I was overcome with suspicion and canceled both appointments. If they were really competent, why weren't they too busy to take me on?

Desperate to put a brake on my madness, I finally took the advice of an elderly neighbor. She was a retired nurse and a level-headed person. I was impressed by the background of her internist. A graduate of Yale Medical School, he had done a residency at Johns Hopkins. What more could I ask for?

The receptionist, greeted us with calm cordiality. "Sorry, but Doctor Berman is covering for another physician today," she explained, "he's forty-five minutes behind schedule. You'll have to wait." So far, I was batting a thousand.

Taking the only vacant seats in the waiting room, Irv lost himself in a magazine. Too nervous to read, I tried to size up the doctor's clientele. Like us, most of them were seniors. Some were very well dressed and looked sophisticated. A few appeared down-at-the-heels. Others were very old and feeble. Watching people fidget impatiently heightened my apprehension.

Eventually, we were the only ones left in the room. Telling us the doctor was ready, the receptionist said Irv was welcome to come with me. Although we joyfully admit to being joined at the hip, both of us hesitated. This was our long-awaited moment of medical truth. But we couldn't face it together. Irv acted as if he were entranced by what he was reading, while I felt reluctant to pull him away.

Dr. Berman turned out to be quite young—not much older than our own children. Yet sadness clouded his face, suggesting that he'd been through the mill. After shaking my hand, he locked his keen brown eyes on mine and began to take a medical history. His manner was firm and forthright. I was struck by his perceptiveness in following up on crucial leads and ferreting out pertinent information. He was no personality kid, but he came across with the warmth of real involvement.

Battling my qualms, I expressed the anxiety I had about the increased frequency of my bowel movements. Responding immediately, he said that any change of this sort could be an indication of trouble. We'd have to set up an appointment for a thorough examination of my lower intestine. "It's probably nothing," I protested. "Maybe I'm taking too much Vitamin C." He was not dissuaded. The only way of being sure was to have the test.

When he began to examine my body, I was comforted by his gentle touch—even as he checked to see if there was any blood in my stool. Fortunately, that test was negative. Then he drew a large syringe of blood for the lab tests. Other doctors often had to poke around to locate the right vein. He slid the needle in quickly and painlessly.

Taking my blood pressure, he frowned as he released the rubber bulb and pumped it up again. My pressure had gone sky high—198 over 90! He asked if I had had this problem before.

"No. When Dr. Stein took it this winter, it was fine."

"That's unusual. Typically, a woman's blood pressure rises when she sees a gynecologist. Lots of patients are sent to me when that happens. We'll have to keep a close eye on you. If it stays so high, you might need medication."

By the time I joined Irv again, I looked as if all the blood from my face had been drained into the test tube the doctor handed to the receptionist. My head whirled from the unexpected appointments she had to set up: one, in two days, for the colon test and another, in three weeks to monitor my blood pressure. To top it off, she reminded me to pick up two Fleet enemas, which I had to take before my next ordeal.

Irv was shaken by my distress. He also shared my doubts about going for the Sygmoidoscopy. Had it been named after Sigmund Freud, we wondered peevishly, to honor his anal phase of psychosexual development? By that evening, however, both of us agreed that the doctor was right to do everything he could to diagnose my complaint.

The exceptionally high level of my blood pressure sent us into a tizzy of speculation. Irv thought it might be due to the strain I had been putting on myself to find the best doctor in Berkshire County. I had to admit that while Dr. Berman was examining *me*, I was making myself extremely tense by trying to evaluate *him*. Was he too young? Too inexperienced? Would I have been better off with the more mature doctor our local librarian recommended?

"Maybe it would be good if you could talk about all this when you see him again. It might help him to understand your reaction."

"Forget it. I wouldn't want to hurt his feelings."

"*His* feelings? Aren't you reversing roles? It's *your* feelings we're trying to figure out."

"You're right…if I really mean what I say about wanting an honest relationship with a doctor."

"At least you could tell him how nervous you were about choosing someone whose judgment you could trust."

"I know. But I'm not sure I have the guts to do it."

Weak from the explosive enemas, I limped into the hospital feeling truly ill. Dr. Berman greeted me sympathetically and explained what he was going to do. He clearly enjoyed using the high-tech equipment and seemed very skilled at it. I felt no discomfort. Everything looked good. But he couldn't get the scope in far enough. It would be necessary to follow up with a barium x-ray.

I was terrified of sinking into a quagmire of complications. As I spoke, my eyes filled with tears and I broke into spasms of convulsive sobbing. I had never let my hair down like this with any other doctor. I felt totally helpless. With no more pride to lose, I muttered that I wanted to talk to him. Tactfully, the nurse left the room.

Alone with him, I haltingly revealed what might have raised my blood pressure. How paranoid I had been. How intently I had tried to psych him out. How depressed I had become about being retired. Completely attuned to my outpouring, he let me ramble on as I revealed how much emotional baggage I had brought into my first visit.

Looking at me without a shred of defensiveness, he said, "I guess we'll both have to learn to deal with your baggage as well as whatever baggage I bring into the situation."

His candor impressed me. Far from being condescending, he was willing to imply that he had some personal problems, too. In spite of my trepidation about the upcoming x-ray, I left the hospital feeling we had established the kind of rapport I needed to feel confident in him.

A few weeks later, I went back to have my blood pressure taken. This time, Irv came into the examining room with me. I had already received a report on the various tests, which were normal, except for a very high cholesterol level. Focusing on that, Dr. Berman emphasized the need to bring it down—way down. I could avoid medication by eliminating fat from my diet and establishing a routine of rigorous exercise, walking five miles or swimming 30–40 laps in a pool—daily.

Hearing five miles, I winced. Was he deliberately proposing more than he expected me to do—like union organizers in a labor dispute bargaining for higher wages than they know they will ever get?

"How about a mile-and-a-half?" I asked meekly. "We have a hilly road along the river bank that's great for hiking."

"Whatever you enjoy. If you don't like the activity, you're not going to do it."

When he broached the issue of losing weight, I gave an excuse for not starting the diet recommended in his letter. "Our grandchildren were visiting."

"Well, your grandchildren weren't stuffing food into your mouth."

Of course not, I thought, I was stuffing food into their mouths.

At last, he took my blood pressure. He was visibly surprised to find it had gone down to 140 over 80. And I hadn't even started to diet or exercise. Looking at each other, Irv and I savored a delicious sense of mutual validation. We were correct in assuming that my initial wariness had led to the rise in my pressure. Maybe I could also succeed in losing weight and lowering my cholesterol count. But there was no doubt that I needed a doctor's help before I could mobilize my own ability to help myself.

# PERFECTLY
# IMPERFECT

Why was I so snotty about Sue's mission to find an internist for *both* of us? So afraid to learn what a medical exam might tell me? Hadn't I always taken professional pride in my readiness to accept ownership of feelings and motives people are generally eager to disavow?

These queries sparked an association to Ernest Becker's book, *The Denial of Death*, where he says people are gods who shit. I couldn't help but laugh when I recalled the outrageous aptness of his definition. But I quickly rejected its application to myself, since I suffered from chronic constipation. Did my difficulty in shitting mean I was only a demigod?

Then it occurred to me that Becker may have unwittingly put the truth in reverse. Maybe he intended to write that we're shits who presume to be gods. That's closer to what I felt about myself when I labored to loosen the drawstrings of my bowels.

I had created the trouble by squeezing much harder than necessary. The hemorrhoids I developed grew larger the more strenuously I squeezed. This swelling, in turn, interfered with the mechanics of defecation. It also provoked me to squeeze more persistently, the better to breach the growing obstruction.

Eventually, I broke my ass with this vicious cycle, inducing rectal bleeding while writhing on the potty. Sometimes this bleeding wracked me with anxiety. Was I having a hemorrhage? What could I do to staunch it?

Approaching all of my evacuations with dread, I tried to calm down with a dose of rationality. After all, even Martin Luther had a legendary case of flaming piles—

and at a much earlier age. That didn't stop millions of people from revering him as their spiritual leader. Why berate myself? I had been defecating for more than sixty years before my ailment became acute. It could have been caused by wear and tear alone. Didn't the sands of time ultimately scour the life out of all the organs in everyone's body?

Surely, the recent changes in my sexual apparatus reflected the heavy imprint of time. Shortly after I turned seventy, my fully erect penis suddenly curved upward in a pronounced arch from root to tip. Even if I were a psychosomatic prodigy, could I have willfully sculpted such an anatomical marvel? My "hook," as we endearingly named it, did not diminish my organ's erotic utility. Sue claimed it gave her new and exciting sensations. Still, we wondered how badly the curvature would get. Would my serviceable crescent become an unwieldy boomerang?

We also noticed I was taking more time to ejaculate. And I needed more genital stimulation to maintain an erection. Sue was happy to accommodate me. Together, we decided to turn my liability into an advantage by lingering longer in the pleasures of foreplay.

As both of us knew, this change in men often begins about the age of fifty. Was it merely a coincidence that my steep ejaculatory decline began with the rising of my hook? Or were they somehow related to a common and treatable malady? These two symptoms were very disturbing. Horror of horrors, they could worsen and wipe out our entire sex life.

Since I had done nothing to generate or foster these difficulties, I didn't feel guilty about them. However, my tormented rear end was quite a different matter. Despite my attempts to consider it a by-product of aging, I couldn't dispel my feeling of being personally responsible for its onset and worsening. That's why I was evading the possibility of a complete physical. I was ashamed to let anyone in the world know about my self-inflicted injury. Although Sue knew, she could be trusted not to reveal my most guarded foibles to others.

Aha, there it was! My abject terror of having a doctor witness the incontrovertible evidence of my imperfection. I didn't want to be humiliated by confessing that it stemmed from my "command performances"—from my insistence on controlling every uncontrollable blip in the workings of my digestive physiology. Because of this demented vanity, I was refusing to get treatment for my hemorrhoids—or for anything else ailing me.

Stretched out in my recliner or hunched over my desk, I spied on Sue's amazing metamorphosis. Day by day, she became more resolute in taking Dr. Berman's advice about changing her diet and getting more exercise. Within a month, she was following her regimen with the diligence of a religious convert.

What astonished me most were her morning walks. Slipping out of bed while I was till comatose, she briskly donned her sweat suit and hiking boots. Before I fully opened my eyes, she was on the back road leading to the Community Center.

Usually, I fell asleep again. Her noisy return woke me up. Stomping and puffing, she marched directly into the bathroom to study the effects of her aerobic excursion. Her face was always beet red, which pleased her immensely—indisputable proof that her blood was circulating nicely. And she beamed with satisfaction each time she stepped on the scale.

Groggily, I would drag myself into the kitchen and find her humming to herself as she prepared breakfast. Extolling the wonders of rapid walking, she emphasized how alive it made her feel; how it got her tuned up to cope with whatever she had to do the rest of the day. Seated at the counter between us, I would huddle into my bulky robe and nod my head. But I denied her the pleasure of vocally applauding her enthusiasm. And I fought to subdue my envy of her willpower.

She looks better than she has for years, I mused. Her figure is slimmer and sexier. Along with her weight, her cholesterol count is down. She stands more upright and her stride exudes a surplus of energy. The gauze of depression has been moved from her shining eyes. Aglow in the aura of her elevated mood, she seems like a full-color ad for Prozac.

It certainly hadn't hurt *her* to admit she needed medical help. Nor did getting it render her a less perfect being. On the contrary, she was vastly improved by going to the doctor. When will I see the light?

I'm a hard nut to crack. Harder and nuttier than I ever wanted to admit to myself. Seriously addicted to perfectionism, a narcotic as accessible and reliable as Alladin's lamp. Constantly rubbing it to smooth out all the rough edges of existence. Yet hadn't I once kicked a pernicious manifestation of this habit—with a doctor's indispensable assistance?

That episode began while Sue and I were in the midst of an incredibly stressful media tour to publicize our first book. In our hotel room, after a traumatic experience on TV, I launched into an outpouring of self-castigation. Why had I permitted us to get snared into the sleazy trap of marketing? To become goofy baboons in pandering to the kind of people who watch talk shows?

When I woke the next morning, I felt a sharp soreness and maddening itch on the right side of my back. Reaching around to touch it, my hand slithered across a sticky goo oozing out of little circles of inflammation. Petrified, I saw myself in the clawing grip of a monstrous plague.

Eventually, my condition was diagnosed as numismatic eczema. True to the name of this weird eruption, I had minted a veritable treasury of coins in different denominations: quarters, nickels, pennies, and dimes. Soon, I spread this slimy wealth to my legs, arms, and hands.

When our tour was over, we came up to Sandisfield for a semester's leave of absence from NYU. We had been looking forward to writing the opening chapters of our marriage book. We also planned to add a bedroom and bathroom to our house. Since my skin was peaking with floridity, we had to put everything aside until I got to a doctor.

The dermatologist I saw quickly dissipated my virulent hypochondria. No bacteria or viruses were attacking me. I was doing the damage all by myself. Ordinarily, Dr. Coleman confided, he wouldn't think of telling most of his patients what he was about to tell me. They didn't have the education or sophistication to make use of it. But I might.

My blemishes, he went on, were outcroppings of a venomous attitude. What was that? The ambition to be perfect. If people like me fall too short of their impossible stipulations in whatever they set their hearts on doing, they begin to pop out of their skin with indignation at themselves.

He would put me on cortisone to relieve my symptoms. This medication was a palliative—not a cure. Because of its side effects, I couldn't stay on it indefinitely. He hoped I would reduce the fury I was heaping on myself and learn to live with my frailties. As I was leaving, he called out, "Remember, Irving, you can't trade yourself in for a new model." In other words, psychologist shrink thyself. Bring your inflated ego down to the size of a mere mortal. Or be prepared for a creepy-crawly future.

On our way home, Sue made a teasing effort to restore my sense of humor. "Maybe you were making so much money on your skin to be sure that our tour wasn't a total loss." I was impervious to her levity. My displeasure with myself persisted through many more visits to Dr. Coleman for checkups. After I stopped taking cortisone, my minting slowly faded. But I wrestled for years with the prescription to accept myself—as is—before letting it sink in enough to limit my perfectionism to occasional and mild outbreaks of eczema.

My self-acceptance was by no means all-embracing. Even as I eased up on the laceration of my skin, I continued to punish other parts of my body for the inability to be faultless. So I sternly chastised my rectum for the failure to defecate with instantaneous perfection.

I was convinced that I had to be seen by a doctor again. Only a literally naked exposure of my folly could help me ameliorate my current sufferings. But when would I reach for the telephone to make an appointment with Dr. Berman?

When the second spring of our retirement arrived, we were much more acclimated to our situation. Thoroughly enjoying our freedom to live and create as we wished, nostalgia for our academic past had lessened. Invigorated from visits to our daughter in Maryland and our son in South Carolina, we anticipated a productive summer.

In contrast to the previous year, Sue was effervescent. She dug into our garden with gusto, raking leaves from the flower beds, transplanting perennials, and putting in new shrubs. Instead of joining in this celebration, I hung around inside the house like a lounge lizard.

Bouncing into the kitchen with a watering can, she saw me lying in a stupor on the couch. "Still kvetching over your extraction?"

"Actually, I'm starting to feel better. The oral surgeon was marvelous. I'm healing faster than he said I would. What really hurts me, though, is that I cracked the tooth myself."

"It wasn't the first time you did it. But you wouldn't listen to the dentist who told you to get a mouth guard against your nightly grinding."

"Naturally, I changed dentists rather than admit I had a habit I couldn't control."

"Naturally."

"I did the same thing I've been doing about seeing an internist. Catering to my false pride, instead of admitting a doctor can help me."

"I'm glad you said it! I haven't been able to get through to you," Sue added as she started walking toward the door.

"Wait! I just got a bolt of insight. It was a wisdom tooth, right?"

"So?"

"Maybe it's the signal I've needed to wise up and make an appointment with Dr. Berman."

"No kidding? You don't want to put it off for a few more years?"

"O.K., give me the business. I deserve it."

Sue set the can on the counter and leafed through the calendar on the wall. "Here. My checkup is still six weeks off. If you call today, you'll probably be able to see him the same morning."

The night before my scheduled visit, I could hardly sleep. Talk about tossing and turning! All the years of my resistance crystallized into a pure geode of terror. Its flashing alarms were unremitting. What would the doctor find in my colon and prostate? Could he do anything to remedy my hemorrhoids? Would he declare me all fucked up, sexually? And what about my heart? Good God, I hadn't given it a thought before.

By 3 AM, I'd made myself so crazed I was sure my blood pressure was in the upper stratosphere. For all I knew, it may have been chronically high since my last physical exam. In a month, I could get myself more ready for it.

On this note of resignation, I lost consciousness. When I woke up, I decided not to cop out. If I did have a terminal illness, medical intervention might give me more time to live. If I didn't, wouldn't that be good news? Besides, I owed it to Sue. I had unfairly burdened her with worry.

We had agreed it would be a growth experience for me to face the doctor on my own. But while waiting in the examining room, I stewed in a cauldron of anxiety. I couldn't focus on any of the lines I had prepared to begin my conversation with him. The moment he stepped into the room, I began a disjointed babble about how scared I had been to come. My sleepless night. My self-destructive perfectionism. My hemorrhoids, my hook, and ejaculatory change. My admiration for how well Sue had done as his patient.

Dr. Berman received this deluge without being swamped. Gazing steadily at me, he showed no hint of impatience. The interest he displayed gave me permission to get out everything I had to say.

When I finished, he asked for some additional information about the symptoms I had described. Then he began a more formal interview, covering the standard items in a medical history.

I was completely relaxed as Dr. Berman began the physical segment of my exam. Thumping, pressing, and listening, he gave every part of my body attentive scrutiny. The verdict: I was in pretty good shape.

Feeling like a born-again kid, I hopped up to the receptionist's desk to make an appointment for a Sygmoidoscopy. Meanwhile, I searched the waiting room for Sue's eyes. Looking up from a magazine, she could see that the doctor had given me a passing grade.

Back in the car, I began a summary of his findings. "My heart is fine and my blood pressure is normal."

"Great! What about your prostate?"

"One side is larger than the other, but it felt alright to him. To be safe, he's doing the blood test you've been after me to get."

"And your pissing?"

"No problem, really. The enlarged prostate just keeps the bladder from emptying completely."

"I saw the receptionist giving you the same form I took to the hospital." A devilish grin spread over Sue's face. "I knew you'd get it up the tushy, too."

"Happy? Now we can literally be ass-hole buddies."

"Was it because of your bleeding?"

"Yeah. But he thinks it all comes from my hemorrhoids. Did you know that at least 70% of the population has them? He prescribed cortisone suppositories to shrink mine. Did you also know people were meant to live in the jungle and can never get too much roughage? He advised a cave man's dosage of Metamucil to end my constipation."

"Now for the Masters and Johnson question. What about your hook?"

"He said it's probably due to a circulatory glitch. He saw no abnormality in my penis."

"Did he think you had to see a urologist?"

"No. He's referred other men in the past and it didn't do them any good. I guess I'll just have to live with it."

"Of course, he still has to examine your colon and get the results of the lab tests."

"But he said…twice…how healthy I look for a man of my age."

"Doesn't it feel good to know you're basically O.K.?"

"It sure does."

"I'm really glad you finally did this for yourself."

"Not only for myself, but for *us*. I was being very unreliable. If something terrible happened to me, you'd be just as badly affected by it."

Quietly, we lapped up the green glory of the countryside. Over every familiar bend in the road, we saw new scenic treasures. No matter how many times we traversed these hills, we would never exhaust their capacity to please us.

I patted Sue's hand gratefully. "Thanks for bearing with me."

"You're very welcome. Who wants to face these things alone?"

"Well, isn't that what it's all about...trusting one another to do the best for both of us?"

# STILL LONGING FOR THE LIMELIGHT

In the course we taught together on human sexual love, many of the students were film majors. It appealed to them because sex was often a prominent theme in their projects. We liked having these students in class. They added pizzazz to the discussions with their unconventional views. Occasionally, an aspiring Spike Lee or Oliver Stone took the initiative to chat with us about some controversial issue. But after handing in their final exams they never came to see us again.

We were very surprised when Raoul O'Connell, who had been in our class over a year before, showed up one day at the end of a lecture. We recognized him immediately. His penetrating questions and incisive comments had made us quite aware of his presence.

Approaching us hesitantly, Raoul said he was in the process of making his first film. "I was wondering if you could lend me a copy of your book, *Masturbation and Adult Sexuality*?" With a lame smile, he went on, "I've lost mine… somehow…somewhere." Then a broad grin erupted on his pixy face. "I want to use it in a scene I'm going to shoot right here in this room."

It sounded as if our course was going to play a big role in his picture. How could we refuse to lend him the book? Our quick exchange of glances yielded a silent consensus. Handing over the copy we always brought to class, Sue asked, "What's the film about?"

"Well, I haven't worked it all out yet." Pausing nervously, he said, "Basically it's about a gay guy looking for love…and I'm going to play the lead."

After he left, Irv smirked. "Raoul is going to push our book to the top of the charts."

"Right. It'll be featured in a student film that may never even get made...much less shown anywhere."

"We can't deny it's flattering to see how much our approach to love has influenced him."

Another year passed before Raoul walked into our class to return the book. Instead of just thanking us and leaving, he began an account of his progress—or rather, his problems. "The work is going well...but much too slowly. I need to raise more money." Sighing, he lamented, "I missed the deadline for a film festival I was hoping to enter."

While he related his woes, we had the feeling he was psyching himself up to ask for something else. Would he dare to hit us up for a financial contribution?

Shifting the weight on his feet and giving us a charming smile, Raoul finally asked, "Would you be willing to do the voice-over I planned as an introduction to the opening scene?"

This was an unusual request for a student to make of his teachers. Placed on the spot, we could hardly discuss our qualms in front of him. We seriously doubted he would ever finish his film. So why bother with it? Yet, assuming the voice-over would contain material from our lectures, the temptation to join his cast began to outweigh our doubts.

"Gee, we'd like to help you out. But...this is our last term at NYU," Sue confessed. "We're retiring...and we'll be up in the Berkshires all summer. Could it wait until the fall? We'll be in the city then…for a while."

"You guys retiring? I can't visualize this course being taught by anyone else. Is this something you want to do?"

"Well, we're conflicted about it," Irv admitted. "But right now, the University's policy makes it mandatory for professors to retire at age seventy."

"Seventy? You can't be that old!" Raoul was astonished, but not upset enough to forget what he wanted from us. "Here's my number. Give me a call when you get back into town." Scribbling on a piece of paper, he added, "In case I move, you can leave a message with my mother at this number in Queens."

Sue managed to retrieve an index card from her bag. Hastily, she wrote down the telephone number and address of our house in the Berkshires. Despite feeling frazzled, she handed it to Raoul with pedagogical aplomb.

On the way to our office, Irv muttered, "That was pretty weird, wasn't it?"

"You mean telling him about our retirement?"

"Yeah…especially after keeping it from all of our present students. And what about agreeing to be in his movie? That was a perfectly normal everyday event for us."

Sue chuckled, "He's going to put our name in lights. With us in there, he can't miss the Academy Awards."

When we returned to New York in the Fall of 1992, the term was up and running. But we couldn't latch on to any of its customary routines. Assailed by the painful deprivation of being out of the academic loop, we felt very sorry for ourselves. We were also having trouble adapting to the limited space of the studio we had rented upon retiring.

Desperate to improve our morale, we decided to call Raoul. Getting an unfamiliar voice on his answering machine, we left a brief message about when and where we could be reached. Worried that he might not get the information, we also phoned his mother and put the same message on her machine. But we didn't hear from either of them before leaving the city two weeks later.

In the middle of October, we were amazed to find a letter from Raoul in the mailbox at our house in the country. It contained a printed invitation to a party aimed at raising money for his film. Video excerpts from the work-in-progress were to be shown.

"Is this kid for real?" Irv asked. "First, he disappears without a trace. Then we get this fancy invitation…like for a Hollywood premier. He's even got Larry Kramer listed as one of his sponsors."

"That's impressive! If Kramer is willing to back up Raoul's movie, he must think it's exceptional for a student film."

Irv kept staring at the invitation. "The party's in Chelsea. We could walk there from our studio. Anyway, we're planning to go into the city soon."

"Never mind the rationalizations. I know you would-
n't want to miss the chance to meet a playwright as
prominent as Kramer."

"What about you?"

"Well, it probably would be fun," Sue conceded. "I'm
curious to see if Raoul actually included a shot of our
book."

Heading for the party on a chilly November night, we
warmed to fantasies of the lively characters who would
be there. But when we stepped into the tightly packed
apartment, we were disappointed by the scene. Far from
being exuberant and exotic, the crowd was restrained
and conventionally dressed. Most of the guests were
middle-aged men who were engaged in quiet conversation.

Suddenly spotting us, Raoul reached out to shake our
hands. "It's great that you could come. I haven't forgot-
ten," he apologized. "I've just had one hassle after
another. I can't locate the recording equipment I need.
As soon as I get it, I'll call you."

"It might have been better for us earlier in the fall,"
Irv replied coolly, reasserting our independence after
having allowed him to take us for granted.

Raoul smiled sheepishly, but with a twinkle in his
eye. "Sorry I never got in touch to explain…I really
hope you can do the voice-over."

Sue quickly expressed our main concern. "We still
have no idea what you expect us to say."

"Don't worry. I'll give you the lines. Excuse me," he muttered, running off.

Just then, we saw Larry Kramer enter the apartment. He looked tired and drawn. We knew he had AIDS. But his movements were quick and intense; his facial expression sensitive and keen. Taking Raoul by the hand, he introduced him to influential friends and acquaintances. Before we could step forward and say anything to Kramer, he called everyone to attention. Presenting Raoul to the gathering, he made laudatory remarks about his artistic promise and the positive contribution his film would make to the gay community.

Raoul clicked on the VCR. Several times, he had to jump up and adjust the tracking. Although the picture was difficult to follow, the audience reacted approvingly, laughing in all the right places. And we thrilled at the scene where Raoul was holding our book.

When the tape was over, a dignified, gray-haired man made a pitch for money. "We've got to support our young artists. This work could help put gay films into the mainstream. It deserves everything we can give."

Recognizing the social implications of what Raoul was doing, our annoyance with him was considerably alleviated. We didn't go so far as to make a donation. But as we left, we gave him our hearty congratulations and sincerely said we looked forward to working with him.

At noon, on a snowy day in February of 1993, Raoul arrived at our studio with a formidable array of recording gadgets. Despite the success of his fund-raising party, he told us it would cost more than he collected to get the sound track he wanted. So the completion of his project was still uncertain.

By the time he unpacked the state-of-the-art taping machine he borrowed from NYU, Raoul had transformed his persona. Ready to do the recording, he exuded the poise of a seasoned director. "O.K., folks," he asserted firmly, "these are your lines."

As we read the pages under his confident scrutiny, we were appalled to see that our parts were vastly different from what we had imagined. Instead of casting us as the teachers we had been, he wanted us to play the roles of his *parents*.

Stunned, we glanced at each other with dismay. "You mean we're supposed to be *other people*?" Irv croaked.

Blinking in disbelief, Sue asked, "So we're not going to be heard lecturing in class?

"No," he said cheerfully, unabashed by her distress. "Trust me. The dialogue is *perfect* for you and Irv. You'll be great!"

Like gently chastised children, we lapsed into the submissive quiet that precedes a reluctant acquiescence. What else could we do? Throw him out? Tell him to find replacements? We had gotten too far into this thing to beg off. Obediently, we capitulated.

Reversing the student-teacher relationship, Raoul demonstrated how we should speak our lines. When he turned on the appropriate switches, both of us clutched up. We weren't surprised that he made us repeat the first recording. After the third reading, however, we began to feel somewhat humiliated. Weren't we doing him an inestimable favor? How could he presume to push us around?

Balking but polite, Irv insisted that Raoul explain why he wanted us to do a fourth version of the dialogue. He obliged with striking expertise. Each reading brought out different strengths in our rendition. He intended to listen to all the versions, select the best-sounding bits, and splice them together for the final tape.

This explanation convinced us of Raoul's competence and commitment to quality. He had the patience and tenacity to settle for nothing less than the very best he could do. No teacher could fail to be impressed by such creative integrity.

Since he made slight changes in the script as we went along, Raoul had all the more reason to ask for additional readings. He kept us going until we had recorded the dialogue seven times. By then, he seemed to feel he had squeezed out every drop of dramatic talent we had to offer.

After he departed, the walls of our studio closed in on us. We had to get out and siphon off the tensions of our "command performance." Striding briskly down West Broadway toward Canal Street, we saw an ominous dark cloud floating up from the south in the dull winter sky. "I hope we're not in for another big storm," Sue remarked.

Back in our apartment, we clicked on the radio to get a weather report. The cloud we saw had nothing to do with the elements. It was a residue of smoke from the bombing of the World Trade Center.

Only a short distance from our place, the tallest pair of buildings in the world had been blasted by terrorists. People were killed and bleeding. Panic was spreading through the city. Totally oblivious to the disaster, we had been taping our immortal words for Raoul's masterpiece. Talk about Nero fiddling while Rome burned!

Over a year later, Sue shattered the morning hush in our apartment. "I can't believe it! Raoul's film is opening at the Quad today!"

Irv rushed out of the bathroom, hands dripping and face smeared with shaving cream. "Let me see," he barked, grabbing the Village Voice spread out on her lap.

"Watch it! You're getting me wet. Here," she pointed, "*A Friend of Dorothy* is included with two other short films in a full-length feature called, *Boys Life*."

"How about that!"

"I guess he's finally making it after all this time. The first show is two o'clock. We've got to go see it."

"Great, let's celebrate our movie debut with a power lunch. From there, we go straight into Spielberg's stable."

"But remember, Irv, no matter what he offers us…we don't do anything but freebies."

We arrived twenty minutes early. Inside, the theater was already quite full. Luckily, we found two adjoining seats with a central view of the screen. Leaning over and cupping her hand around Irv's ear, Sue whispered, "Did you notice? I'm the *only woman* in the whole place!"

"I guess women are also capable of sexism."

"You'd think there'd be at least a few female film-makers interested in checking out what these guys have done."

"But it's really impressive to see the place packed with so many men on a workday afternoon," Irv said. "A lot of them look like corporate types."

"Yeah," Sue agreed, nodding discreetly toward the man clad in an elegant suit who was sitting in front of us playing backgammon on a laptop computer.

At last, the house lights dimmed and *Boys Life* went on. Since Raoul's film was second on the program, we had to contain our impatience. When the first picture ended, we peered into the darkness for the credits introducing his opus. Instead, the screen remained black, except for an occasional flicker from the projector rolling out the blank film. Meanwhile, *our* recorded voices began to fill the theater.

We were discussing our "son's" shyness and his imminent enrollment as a freshman at NYU. Sue, "the mother," was protective of the boy, saying she worried about him being lonely.

Irv, "the father," expressed anxiety about letting the boy go to college "in the Village."

This line drew a brief laugh from the audience. But what really broke them up was when Irv—with just the right intonation—blurted out why his son didn't have any friends: "He's always up in his room listening to Barbra Streisand."

Unlike the distraught father, the men roaring around us knew this was an inside joke. Judy Garland is also a beloved icon. Her portrayal of Dorothy in *The Wizard of Oz* has led many a gay man to depict himself as "a friend of Dorothy"—the code words Raoul used as the title of his picture.

Pumped up by the effect of our dialogue, it took us some time to focus on what was happening in the film. Raoul was frantically searching for true love everywhere on the campus—his dorm, the library, and Washington Square Park. His misadventures delightfully mixed poignancy with comedy, while his performance in the leading role was polished and engaging.

Dawdling on the way home, we clung to the idea that we were in a movie at the very theater where we had previously been only members of the audience. Of course, our fellow viewers had no way of knowing we were the "parents" in the voice-over. But their sustained applause at the end of the film, made us feel wonderful about having done our acting stint.

"The shot of our book showed up very well," Irv enthused. "You could really read our names on the cover. Maybe we should get a bunch of copies and stand outside to sell them after every show."

"That's all we have to do with ourselves. But I must admit, the film is much better than anything we expected. It's going to be a hit."

"No question about that. Judging from the reaction today, it'll be here for weeks. What a break for Raoul!"

Sue frowned a little. "He could have had the decency to call us Mom and Dad in the credits at the end of the film. Or Mother and Father, at least. *Not* Ma and Pa. That's what our kids called their *grandparents*." Pressing closer, she tightened her grip on Irv's arm. "It made me feel so ancient."

"Poor thing…can't keep up with the young folks anymore."

"Quit it! I know we've never had to take the kind of risk these guys did by making their first film about their own coming out. But it's been pretty heavy for us to bow out of teaching and…"

"And do it gracefully?"

"As Andy Warhol might have said, we've had our few minutes in the sun. Big deal! Nobody in the theater knew who we were."

"So what. We got our kicks," Irv shrugged. "Besides, we have the satisfaction of knowing we helped to produce something worthwhile."

"Life is funny…isn't it? As a little girl, I was such a chatterbox. Whenever I tried to open my mouth at the dinner table, my father shut me up with 'children should be seen but not heard'."

"Well, at our age, it's nice to be heard…even if we can't be seen."

# DANCING ON OUR GRAVES

Quite appropriately, the main burial ground in our town is located just up and across the road from the dump, which was recently renamed "the transfer station." The cemetery transfers the erstwhile living to the discarded dead. But there, the similarity ends. While the dump is cloaked in the shadows of a rather cramped spit of land, the cemetery spreads over a large and sunlit hillside. From its lofty slopes, there is an uncluttered view across a wide and forested valley. The blend of evergreens and deciduous trees provides a constantly changing panorama as the leaves on the hardwoods turn from silvery wine in early spring to soft chartreuse in May and emerald green at the summer's height. Autumn erupts in a heroic blaze of gold, red, and orange, before the proud limbs bare themselves to the coldness of the winter light. If this place were for sale as a home site, it would be considered a very desirable piece of property.

We passed the cemetery every time we went out of town to shop. It was a familiar sight, evoking no particular interest. But after our retirement, Irv got into the habit of stealing a leftward glance to survey the sprawling graveyard. With the morning sun shining on their backs, the silhouettes of the scattered headstones loomed dark and forbidding.

It was a more cheerful sight on our return trip. Slowing down at the cross-road before our descent, Irv moved the shift into second gear, turned off the overdrive, and let the car glide down toward the valley. Now, he looked surreptitiously to the right, his eyes more glowing than glazed. Sue was also struck by the transformation the afternoon had performed. Reflecting the hot pink of the setting sun, the gravestones seemed to have come alive, offering an almost tempting invitation to bury one's worldly cares beneath them.

But eventually, Irv's unmistakable preoccupation exasperated her. "What's your thing with the cemetery?"

"I feel I'm running out of time. I'm losing patience for putting things on hold. So I've been thinking…if we like this town enough to own a house and land here, why not be buried here?"

"You're getting morbid. Are we really ready to drop dead tomorrow? Anyway, we have a place waiting for us in the large family plot your father bought on Long Island."

"Yeah, and he got it long before he died. But we never liked Long Island or wanted to move there. Our kids don't live anywhere near it. I'll be damned if I'll let myself be put out there…even if it upsets my brothers. You know our children and grandchildren will use the homestead here after we're gone. If we're lucky, they'll come by and leave a stone on our graves once in a while."

"It all seems so far off and unreal," Sue protested.

At a loss for a rationally convincing answer, Irv aimed at her sense of thrift. "Listen, we can get a four-grave plot for $100. Where else could we find such a bargain? It's a fantastic deal! The same piece once cost only $25. Who knows when the price will go up again?"

"Well, why don't you do it, instead of just thinking about it? I'm sick of your obsession. If you keep on staring at the goddamn place every time we go by, you'll go off the road and put us in a plot before you even have a chance to buy one!"

After that confrontation, she agreed to visit the cemetery and scout around for a suitable location. Why not, she figured. Maybe, if I go along on his trip, I'll get the nut case off my back. And he'll get the madness out of his system.

Rattled by the vehemence of her sarcasm, Sue realized how defensive she had been about coming to grips with mortality. Obviously, I've been masking my own anxiety by criticizing Irv. Maybe he's right. My parents died at a much earlier age than his. Being "the baby" in my family, I've always regarded myself as an ingenue. But now, at my stage of life, hasn't my act lost its credibility? How much longer can I go on denying my fear of death?

We drove to the upper reaches of the cemetery before parking. Always suckers for a grand vista, we had paid a lot of rent in Manhattan for the privilege of looking through windows twenty-one floors above the street. Here we were, in the bucolic Berkshires, still striving to be King and Queen of the hill—forevermore.

Getting out of the car, we filled our lungs with the fresh summer breeze blowing in from the west. The sky was so clear and blue we could see intimations of the Infinite shining through. So far, so good.

We started to wander among the graves. Where, in the unused vastness of this mortal terminal, do we wish to be stashed away? Only the uppermost part of the cemetery was already filled. Evidently, other people also wanted the highest elevation for their descent into the earth. But there was still plenty of room near the top for us to be quite elevated—if not on the very apex of the heap.

As we surveyed the unclaimed land, we were reminded of an incongruous fact of the afterlife here. Unlike the living in our township, where Christians and Jews intermingle with a remarkable degree of harmony, the dead are strictly separated along religious lines. Having attended some local funerals, we knew that the cemetery was divided into two parts: Christian (large) and Jewish (small) in rough proportion to the size of those groups in the community.

In keeping with the town's libertarian ethos, this sectarian division did not originate with the Christian majority. Long ago, rabbis had decreed that they would not officiate unless the deceased were interred in specially sanctified ground. So a portion of the cemetery was set aside for that purpose. But many of the Jewish inhabitants had gone elsewhere for their truly permanent residences. To this day, the Jewish segment is sparsely populated with headstones. Its forlorn ambiance is accentuated by a chain-link fence at the summit and a dirt road on the side facing the remains of our Christian neighbors.

Staring glumly at these unsightly barriers, we remarked that the whole scene—with its Stars of David here and its Crosses over there—was out of keeping with the spirit of the town. Indeed, the unique appeal it holds for us is its freedom from conformity. Here, we feel more at liberty to be ourselves than we do anywhere else but on the island of Manhattan. We can socialize with whomever we wish—and not worry about what people might say or think. Or, we can remain sequestered for weeks on end—and emerge to be welcomed by anyone we choose to see again. Feeling no pressure to keep up, down, or sideways with the Joneses, we can watch the dandelions sprout over our lawns and let our rock walls slide slowly into disarray.

Ironically, after years of opposing all forms of discrimination, we agreed to accept—in death—the kind of segregation we had fought in conducting our lives. As this ridiculous social reality sank in, we felt consoled by a very funny notion: Sandisfield is more progressive than Long Island. If we were buried in Mount Ararat with Irv's family, there wouldn't be a Christian in sight.

We stepped onto the nicely trimmed grass and began examining every feature of the terrain. Occasionally, we sounded out our reactions to a particular locale. Irv came up with the first suggestion—a plot near the fence. That would give us the highest elevation. Despite her own attraction to the heights, Sue rejected the idea without any hesitation. "You're not going to get me near that ugly thing."

"But think of the view."

"No way! Can't you see it's a *link* fence? It would be different if it was a split-rail. *That*, I could live with."

Considering this option firmly closed, she continued to move downward. Irv followed her meekly. Hadn't he pushed for this little jaunt into the macabre? The least he could do was to make it as pleasant as possible.

He broke his silence as he saw another likely spot. "Hey, what about here?"

"Are you crazy? It's too far from the road. The kids would have to tramp through too much snow to reach us."

Returning to the hunt, Sue made a proposition of her own. "What about this one?"

"Hell no! That's so close to the road it feels claustrophobic. Forget it!"

With this exchange, both of us were struck by the grotesque absurdity of our quest for the perfect grave site. Overcome by our weirdness, Irv let out a whoop and started hopping and skipping. Sue picked up the rhythm without missing a beat. Together, we improvised some hysterical rocking and rolling. Running out of breath, we held hands and collapsed under a convulsion of laughter.

That evening, we called the cemetery supervisor—who doubles as chief gravedigger—to finalize a purchase.

"Hi, Tony," Irv began brightly, "we were over to the cemetery today."

"Oh, yeah?" he replied flatly.

"Yup, we tried it on for size."

After a hearty guffaw, Tony said, "I guess you want to buy a plot. O.K., I can meet you there tomorrow morning at ten."

When we arrived, we found Tony leaning against the cab of his half-ton truck, which he had parked on the road adjoining the Jewish section. Besides overseeing the real estate of the cemetery, he's a major landholder in town and has a lucrative business in plumbing and construction.

We had met Tony soon after buying our house and had developed very mixed feelings for him. We felt grateful for his help when our furnace went out in a blizzard and our basement was flooded by rampaging rains. Yet we were resentful that he once seemed willing to let us freeze in sub-zero weather by failing—despite repeated pleas—to deliver fuel oil for our nearly empty tank.

We sensed just as strong an ambivalence on his part. He admired us for writing books and teaching together at NYU. Besides, he had seen us being interviewed on television. Whenever we encountered him at the general store, he loudly announced, "Here come the celebrities." But he also tended to put us down as city slickers who were incapable of surviving in this wilderness without help from guys like him. Now, seeing the bemused smile on his rugged face, we felt he was finally getting the chance to put us in our place—figuratively and literally.

Motioning to us, Tony unfurled a detailed blueprint of the area. He pointed out the available plots and commented on their various advantages. As we pondered our grisly choices, he admired his own family mausoleum, an imposing edifice that sat front and center on the pinnacle of the Christian side of the cemetery. Dwarfing all the other structures, it proclaimed the eminence of his clan.

But age is the ultimate leveler, flattening the elderly into an identical ribbon of black crepe as they mourn the irretrievable loss of their youth and, in realistic anticipation, the implacable loss of their lives. Having come into the world at about the same time, Tony and Irv were equally plagued by the question of when they would depart from it. While they spoke amiably about the layout of the cemetery, each wondered if he would be lucky enough to live longer than the other.

Irv tormented himself with the thought that he would be the first to "go." In that case, he fretted, Tony might still be fit enough to work the backhoe and dig my grave. Then, he could enjoy watching me being lowered into the pit. Making an abrupt switch in his mind, Irv imagined Tony going first. Now, he exulted mutely, I'd be around to attend his funeral. Unfortunately, I wouldn't be able to dig his grave. But I could get a mean and nasty kick out of seeing the dirt cover his casket.

As if tuned into Irv's lethal wavelength, Tony gave voice to his own grim ruminations. "Don't worry," he bantered, "if I'm dead, my son can do the job for you. I've taught him how."

Disarmed, Irv surrendered in this ghoulish game of one-upmanship. "Boy, you don't leave anything to chance. But who knows, maybe I'll go before you."

While quietly witnessing this jousting between Irv and Tony, Sue's own mood was darkening under a cloud of negativity. As she scoured the hillside, frantically wishing for a mystical marker to jump up from the "best" plot, her brain raced with panic. Never mind which one of *them* will go first! What about Irv and *me*?

Of course, I want to go on living as long as I can. Does that mean I hope to outlive him? How can I bear the guilt of such a desire, no matter how understandable it is? Maybe he would be better off if he died before me. After all, how could he manage? Who would do the cooking, pay the bills, keep everything organized, and, most of all, love him? Even if he could handle the practicalities of daily life, he'd die of loneliness.

Distraught from these gruesome visions, she stopped to rest on an attractive patch of turf. Who am I kidding? Am I so indispensable? If I die before Irv, plenty of love-starved women would come crawling out of the woods, only too happy to be of service to him.

God, how can I think of such things? I'd be as devastated if he died before me. Without him, it would be a living death. If I didn't wither away from depression, I'd go into a manic fugue... running from one friend to another...trying to fill the void left by the loss of his love. Without Irv's wisdom and perspective, I'd lose my judgment and make bad decisions. Mainly, who would cuddle up against me at night? And make love to me during the day?

A widower would have a better chance of finding such solace. But it would be much tougher for an old widow like me. I can't deny the unflattering changes in my appearance. The puffiness under my eyes, the brown spots popping out on my skin, the unruly dryness of my whitening hair. Lately, I'm so susceptible to stress…quick to explode in anger at the slightest rebuff or burst into tears when I feel inadequate. Who would want such a shrek?

Nudged out of her reverie by the touch of Irv's hand on the nape of her neck, Sue greeted his gesture with a smile, happy to abandon her secret agitation.

"You've finally found the right spot."

"Do you really think this is it?"

"Well, you seem to like it. You've been sitting here spaced out for quite a while."

"It does feel pretty good. Just far enough from the road to avoid traffic congestion but not so far to be blocked by snow. And from here, you get a lovely view of the distant ridge."

"Great." Taking her hand, he shouted, "Hey, Tony, this is the one we want!"

Comparing our feeling for the parcel with the diagram Tony showed us, we shared a pleasurable sense of satisfaction. Still, we walked the perimeter of our acquisition over and over, putting our personal stamp on the ground.

As he wrote down the number of our plot in his big black book, Tony approved of our decision. "This is a good one. Much better than way up on the top of the hill. You know," he confided, his eyes squinting and his voice becoming a spectral whisper, "it gets mighty cold up there in the winter. One time, it was so bad while I was waiting for a coffin to come from the funeral parlor, I had to jump into the open grave to keep warm."

Our lighthearted laughter released us from the tenacious strain of our mission. We shook hands with Tony and, in the custom of our town, wished one another a nice day. Watching as he drove down the hill, we lingered on—as if so momentous a transaction needed to be drawn out to a finality beyond any residual doubts or misgivings.

Sue took Irv's hand and we began to walk toward our car. "Everything O.K., honey?"

"I guess…At least we're fully prepared now."

"Yeah. Let's hope it works like carrying an umbrella to ward off the rain."

978-0-595-34290-7
0-595-34290-6

www.ingramcontent.com/pod-product-compliance
Lightning Source LLC
Chambersburg PA
CBHW061304280526
45784CB00002B/884